ALTERED AMBITIONS

ALTERED AMBITIONS

WHAT'S NEXT IN YOUR LIFE?

BY DR. BETSY JAFFE

DONALD I. FINE, INC. NEW YORK

Library of Congress Cataloging-in-Publication Data

Jaffe, Betsy.
Altered ambitions : what's next in your life? / Betsy Jaffe.
p.   cm.
ISBN: 1-55611-266-1
1. Career changes.   2. Career development.   I. Title.
HF5386.J32   1991
650.1—dc20   90-56074
CIP

Manufactured in the United States of America

10   9   8   7   6   5   4   3   2   1

Designed by Irving Perkins Associates

To my husband, Mort Jaffe,
and in memory of my parents,
Bill and Jinny Latimer,
for their encouragement of my many
altered and evolving ambitions.

Contents

Acknowledgments

There have been many key players in *Altered Ambitions'* journey to publication. My undying gratitude goes to Anne Edelstein, my agent, who helped shape and reshape and focus the original proposal, then enthusiastically stuck with me through numerous rewrites and setbacks. To Ruth Halcomb, who came to my rescue with miraculous writing and editing skills, lifelong friendship and bicoastal phone calls, which polished and clarified the many new concepts herein—my eternal esteem and affection. My special thanks to Lisa Healy, Executive Editor at Donald I. Fine, for instantly grasping *Altered Ambitions'* messages and shepherding the book deftly to print.

For being my team of advisers, critics, and valued supporters, much appreciation to Susan Dresner, Lorna Pokart, Laurie Norris and Patricia Brill. For their professional wisdom and guidance with the original research, I am indebted to Drs. Jack Mezirow, Walter Sindlinger, Baila Zeitz and Adela Oliver. My particular regard and recognition to those whose work contributed to the evolution of my thinking—Ned Herrmann, Richard Bolles, John Crystal, and the writings of Gail Sheehy, Drs. Roger Gould, Nancy Schlossberg, Daniel Levinson, Paula Robbins, Margaret Hennig and Anne Jardim. *Altered Ambitions* builds on and takes issue with their theories and the foundations they laid.

Finally, my most heartfelt love and thanks to my life partner, Mort Jaffe, my family, friends, clients, colleagues, students and the women in my research, all of whom contributed to my learning so I could pass it on to you.

Betsy Jaffe, April, 1991

xiii

Setting the Stage

WHY THIS BOOK?

Is your life different from what you expected at eighteen, twenty-five, thirty, even sixty if you're there? When I ask women this question, I usually get a resounding "Yes!" If you're like most women, your dreams and ambitions have altered along the way.

There's been a whirlwind of change in the past fifteen years in almost every aspect of our lives—careers, relationships, our view of ourselves, our health, our culture and life-styles.

Major shifts in demographics, the economy, technology, global competition, organizational structures and people's values are complicating our lives and changing the goals we can realistically expect to achieve.

Nothing is as structured or predictable as we expected. Women's lives are now more complex than when we first defined our ambitions or made our five- and ten-year plans. Even with our hard-won degrees, our knowledge is rapidly out-of-date. Outside forces intrude upon our plans and we're caught in a crunch that often seems beyond our control. Nothing is clear-cut anymore.

We can no longer count on lifetime employment at one or two companies or even in a single occupational field. Older, more rigid ways of thinking about work are hazardous to our standard of living. To stay ahead, we need a new, more fluid view of what the future holds. We need to plan for uncertainty.

Life-style priorities count more than ever too. Women, and increasingly men, resist transfers and promotions rather than leave the cities where they've put down roots. Both resist long hours away from their families, too. We know there's more to life than working, and more and more, employers are recognizing this as well. But the complexity of planning for personal priorities often demands greater flexibility.

Women in particular are designing new shapes and patterns in their lives. **More than ever, our personal lives and our careers cannot be put into separate boxes, but are inextricably intertwined, each affecting the other.** We are now playing different roles in series or creating new combinations of roles. For some time, women have been not only responding to change, but pioneering changes of their own with new ambitions and attitudes.

Where do you, as an individual, fit into all this? How can you think critically and globally while having the life-style you want?

These are the questions this book addresses.

HOW TO USE THIS BOOK

Altered Ambitions is meant to be a resource for anyone who is undergoing change or crisis or who anticipates such upheavals. It is addressed especially to working women who feel pressured by the media to "have it all," yet are disappointed that their achievements don't match the ambitions they once set for themselves. Instead of urging you to "have it all," *Altered Ambitions* guides you in developing insights, strategies and coping skills to get the things that matter *most* to you as an individual.

Altered Ambitions distills new research in ways you can apply to your own situation. Acting as a coach, as I do with my clients, I encourage you to see the "Big Picture" and think strategically while dealing with change and projecting your future. You'll also learn how your coping style and your perception of events shape every aspect of your life.

In addition, I've provided exercises to help you pull together what you're learning in the book so you can make the most informed decisions in all aspects of your life. Of the many exercises I use with my clients, I've selected ones they found the most enlightening and useful. The exercises are in a sequence designed to support you as you move through the change process. Each takes ten minutes or less to complete. You'll do better and feel better about your situation as you complete them.

I also use specific stories from the lives of five women to illustrate important points. These five are not actual interviewees. I've used composites in order to protect the privacy of those who participated in my research. But I've taken pains to see that they're not disembodied case histories. They're as realistic as I could make them because I want you to relate to them, empathize with their experiences and learn from them. Their life-span sagas demonstrate my theories on change, coping styles and effective problem-solving strategies.

This book is intended to guide you as you navigate changes in your life, a process that is challenging, often bumpy and always complex. *Altered Ambitions* is the culmination of what I've discovered about how professional men and women cope effectively with change. **It is designed to help you understand yourself better in relation to the world outside, and to help you be more flexible, savvy and open when change occurs.** For no matter what your work, ultimately, the purpose is to enable you to set ambitions that are achievable and to get more of the things you want in your life.

BACKGROUND

In the mid-1970s I sat in the audience as Gail Sheehy spoke to mid-career Harvard MBAs. *Passages* was her topic. Looking out at the audience, she apologized for not having included women's life changes in her remarks. She had expected an all-male audience. At least twenty-five percent were women!

A few years later, I left my fifteen-year career as a department store buyer manager in retailing to become part of the senior management team at Catalyst, the national career development organization for women. For five years I led focus groups there, worked with CEO's to add executive women to corporate boards, and counseled hundreds of educated working women just beginning to question their career directions. Unlike mid-life men, this latter group of women were much younger and reevaluating their lives for different reasons. They were drastically in need of savvy advice on organizational environments and politics, discrimination and surviving as tokens. My consulting practice, teaching, research and writing grew out of my awareness of their needs.

In 1982 I founded my company, Career Continuum, and began doctoral research at Columbia University Teachers College on how women's lives and careers are different from men's. My research revealed that professional women's careers and life paths differ from traditional women's and from men's. Compared to men, the professional women had more moves up and down, more multiple careers, more variation in types of jobs, also different entry points and different sequences. This research planted the seeds for *Altered Ambitions*.

The subjects of this initial research were women between supervisor and superwoman with titles such as manager, director and vice president. I selected a group of twenty-nine of them from hundreds I'd met at Catalyst in the late seventies. They ranged in age from early thirties to early fifties when I first interviewed them. All were college educated and a few had Ph.D.'s. They weren't necessarily oldest children, mentored by their fathers, as the first wave of executive women tended to be. They came from all kinds of families and socioeconomic backgrounds. All had at one time worked for large organizations with offices in New York, but most came from elsewhere and many moved to other geographic areas over the decade that I continued to track them.

During this same period, many corporations began restructuring and downsizing. Women and men who'd spent decades at the same company were suddenly out on the street. Women who'd launched their careers so hopefully a few years earlier were often the first to receive pink slips. **Now a whole new wave of women are rethinking their ambitions, shifting to new fields, starting businesses, having babies and pioneering new career tracks.** These are women who were career-minded, focused and confident when they started out. A few reached the upper rungs of the ladder as they'd hoped, but many faced ceilings, discrimination and pressures they hadn't anticipated. Many, including some who scaled the higher levels, found themselves bored, no longer challenged or with interests that had changed. **The vast numbers of women whose ambitions have shifted and the extent of the changes they've undergone prompted my writing of *Altered Ambitions*.**

This book is a synthesis of my doctoral research, my work at Catalyst with over 1,200 women executives, and my counseling experience. I've counseled some 1,500 women and men, including accountants, attorneys, financial analysts, human resource professionals, marketing specialists and line managers, from both the public and private sectors, from all parts of the country. I've guided them through a process of making new choices and charting new directions for their lives.

Altered Ambitions brings together ideas from many sources. I've consulted psychologists, executives in search and outplacement firms, directors of career change and human resource programs, and career counselors. My audiences of professionals and my graduate students have contributed too.

Some insights came from unexpected corners as well. One of the most important is: **Always be ready to learn, for this is how we survive the worst and create our own destiny.**

ALTERED
AMBITIONS

Seeing the Big Picture

TRENDS THAT ALTER AMBITIONS AND OPTIONS

Most of us fail to see the winds of change that are sweeping our lives, causing our crises, reshaping our plans. **We have tunnel vision when we confront a crisis.** We blame ourselves, look for signs that it might not be true and try to fix whatever went wrong without looking very far in any direction. Not seeing this bigger picture leads us to wrong interpretations and unsound moves.

If you're experiencing any kind of problem in this era of rapid change, it helps to stand back and see the larger context in which that problem occurs. You'll soon see that you're not alone and you'll eventually understand the extent of the trend. **The broader your understanding of these trends, the more realistic you can be in revising your ambitions.**

Let's look briefly at five types of trends that shape who we are and force us to change. As you read, think about how each affects you and your future.

Demographic Trends:
You're Nobody's Baby Now!

The era in which you were born can affect your view of the world, how you cope with your changes and the realities of the job market. Maybe you were a depression-era baby, coming into the world at a time when fewer people were born. Getting into a good college was easier, and so

1

was finding a job when you were first out of school. Habits of thrift you learned growing up may still be noticeable. You may be careful with credit, preferring to pay as you go.

Most likely you're a Baby Boomer, one of the seventy-five million Americans born between 1946 and 1964, one out of every three of us. If so, you're better educated and have greater expectations and different values from previous generations. You were raised in an era of prosperity. The only ceiling was the limit of your own abilities and aspirations, or so you thought. Yet the opportunities fail to match your numbers. You've had to compete harder for jobs, and now that you're in middle management, you may find yourself stuck at a career plateau. You're nobody's baby now.

You're less willing to accept the earlier belief that work is just something to be tolerated. You want your professional life to be satisfying, and you'll switch jobs if you don't like what you're doing or where the company sends you.

After 1964 came the Baby Bust and a whole other view of the world. Fewer babies were born then, partially because the birth-control pill ushered in smaller families, there were fewer depression-era women having children and women's careers became increasingly important. If you are a product of this generation and just starting your career, you worry about many industries being unstable and about your education being quickly outdated. You wonder if you'll ever enjoy your parents' standard of living.

The gender mix in demographics affects ambitions too. Most of us once assumed we'd find a life partner. In today's social climate, however, commitments from men are harder to obtain and sustain. None of us expects to divorce, but women who do may notice that men are scarce. Divorce leaves as many unattached men as women, but men typically chose younger women as partners.

We heard a few years ago that beyond a certain age, a woman's chance of finding a husband was about the same as being abducted by a terrorist. This statistic has since been questioned, but many women who'd hoped for marriage are going it alone and so have more energy to devote to careers and other areas of their lives. Left to their own devices, they've banded together in professional networks and social groups.

Economic Trends

In the eighties, the economic upheaval of merger mania, corporate restructuring, divestiture and heavy leveraged buyout debt wrecked many careers. Close to ten million manufacturing jobs were eliminated and over three million managers were laid off in the eighties. A total of forty percent of the population moved in just five years! Outplacement services for helping laid-off workers became a thriving industry.

Our ambitions became colored by fears for our own survival. Career commitment and loyalties were suddenly not as important anymore. Few people now view the corporation as the safe harbor it once seemed.

Along with increased uncertainty about careers come new ways of working. More and more workers began carving out niches for themselves outside the corporation. Entrepreneurism began growing in the early eighties and hasn't let up yet. Small businesses, franchises and far-flung corporate networks all offer new options and opportunities. **It's now possible to put together a career that better matches your ambitions and yet is less vulnerable to changes in the marketplace.** It's essential, in fact.

Economic trends hit us from another angle as well—the cost of living. Some middle-class women worked for personal fulfillment in the seventies, but today's escalating costs of housing, medical care and education make two incomes necessary. One couple in five cannot keep up with their parents' standard of living.

Single mothers are apt to have the toughest situation of all. A divorced woman undergoes downward mobility as she juggles alone what two adults previously handled. No matter how hard she works, she'll still earn forty-two percent less than her male peers.

Global Competition

The global village is here. In the eighties offshore labor helped to cut costs and to compete with imports. Perhaps your company increased manufacturing abroad, or is owned by overseas investors.

Global markets have risen like a tidal wave. In the seventies a corporation might settle for a large United States market share, while today the goal is to be a major player in global markets. Small companies have grown global. Whole new industries are marketing around the world. Perhaps you're in one or want to be.

With computers linking international financial markets, trading extends to twenty-four hours a day, and ownership of companies becomes constantly more diverse. United States companies have taken partners from all over the world.

Trade barriers are falling like so many bowling pins and as Europe opens its national boundaries, new consortia are formed within industries and between countries, often with previous rivals and the most bitter of enemies. Trade is now the glue holding together diverse parts of the world in ever more complex arrangements of debt and ownership. Through trade and environmental issues, we're beginning to recognize how interconnected we all are.

The global village means many more opportunities, especially for individuals who are not entrenched in old ways and who can be sensitive to cultural differences. **A total of three million new managers with new competencies will be needed by the year 2,000. There is room for more heightened ambitions. Are you ready?**

Technological Trends

Predictably, the high-tech boom has altered every aspect of our lives. One result is that everything is speeded up. Sometimes this makes our lives easier, but not always. Access to data is virtually instant, and much more information is placed in front of us. A new competency is called for in managing all this information, sorting out what's critical and what isn't.

Technology has also brought about new relationships between companies and employees. Many workers are more independent of their employers. Rather than hire people as full-fledged employees with salaries and fringe benefits, companies have allowed for a vast gray area of independent contractors, vendors, free-lancers and others. The Conference Board, a research organization, estimates there are thirty-five million such contingency workers.

Women are pioneers in breaking down old barriers and building the portable workplace. Almost 15.5 million corporate employees, many of them women, are stationed at home, with computers linking them to their companies. In the next few years over thirty million workers are expected to be home-based either full- or part-time.

Surviving in the high-tech world means learning new skills. This makes certain job changes or reentry into the work force harder. **What skills the future will demand is less predictable.** But one thing is certain, **they must be portable—across companies, professional fields and sectors of the economy.**

Sociological Trends

In the seventies women and minorities entered the work force with hopes that the inequities of the past would soon be rectified. In the next decade, however, ninety percent of *Fortune* 500 companies received complaints of sexual harassment. Discrimination became more subtle.

In *The Best Companies for Women*, Baila Zeitz and Lorraine Dusky cite evidence of how little progress we've made. Women and minorities are still relegated to staff jobs, evaluated by different standards, discriminated against, left out of key meetings and held back by successive glass ceilings, they report.

Although changing demographics hold hope for the future, older values in large organizations are still holding women back. Many women are leaving their corporate jobs, some to join smaller firms run by more egalitarian bosses (often minorities or women) and some to start independent operations of their own. Surveys show their reason was "lack of opportunity" in corporations.

On the home front, roles and relationships have changed greatly. **When two spouses work, the careers of both are important.** Today's husbands are more likely to help with homemaking chores and with children. Companies are now more likely to have parental leave, help with relocation and child care to accommodate the two-career family.

As a society, we're growing older and we're growing up. Our priorities are changing. We're turning away from the competitiveness, materialism and glitz of the eighties. We've stopped confusing standard of living with quality of life. We've ceased craving more of everything and want our lives to add up to something worthwhile. We're concerned about safeguarding the earth's resources, distributing them more fairly and preserving them for future generations.

Each of these trends has added to the complexity of our lives, altering our ambitions. Our times are less simple, innocent and monolithic than two decades ago. We need to keep our eyes on the bigger picture, even as it changes. We must, as encouraged in John Naisbitt's *Megatrends*, learn to practice environmental scanning and become trend spotters, not only for the work we do, but for our personal lives too.

We need to keep asking ourselves, "What does this mean for the future? What does this mean for me?" as new information floods in. Instead of waiting passively, then reacting to change after we're at a crisis point, we need to be proactive in our planning, always armed with contingency plans, always flexible. While we can't always travel on a fixed track, we *can* choose our direction. We may not have certainty about the future, but we *can* be more informed as we face it with confidence in ourselves. We *can* reshape our lives, if we're open and willing to learn.

Certain trends have already had an impact on your life and ambitions, and will continue to do so. The chapters that follow will help you clarify where you've been, where you fit into the big picture, and what issues are most important in your future.

PART I

COPING WITH CHANGE

Part I is about coping with the many changes that swirl through our lives, altering our ambitions and sometimes threatening our equilibrium as well.

We'll first look at lives in crisis through the eyes of five women who are typical of professional women today. We'll also look at the types of change most likely to impinge on women's lives, and at two very different ways that people perceive and respond to change.

In the second chapter, you'll have a chance to identify your coping style, so that you can get to know yourself better and pinpoint your individual strengths and weaknesses. Then you'll be introduced to some practical steps for getting through a crisis—any crisis—and valuable resources you can tap for help at such times too.

This first part of the book provides a foundation for facing the future, uncertain as it may be, with considerably more confidence. Subsequent parts of the book will cover how you can shape your life around certain key issues (careers, relationships and health) and finally how to plan for a future with ambitions that are attainable.

CHAPTER I

Lives in Crisis— Yours and Theirs

THE ancient Greeks defined "crisis" as a decisive moment or turning point. If you're like most women today, you've already met the challenge of these kinds of radical changes. Perhaps you've had difficult, even heartbreaking experiences that you never want to repeat or even remember. Perhaps you're in the midst of a crisis or turning point right now.

This chapter will help you take the broader, life-span perspective you need to understand these changes. We'll look at the process of change itself with all its ups and downs. You'll learn how your perceptions and perspective affect how you cope. You'll also meet five women who'll appear throughout the book. Here they are, each at a major crisis in her life.

Elinor loved her retailing job and the future seemed bright. Everything was on schedule when, without warning, her company was sold and sliced into pieces. Shortly after, she was fired. Besides the trauma, she had debts to cope with while looking for work. She didn't know what her next step would be.

Diana, mother of one and hoping to have another child, had always enjoyed good health. After a regular checkup, the gynecologist told her she would need surgery to prevent the spread of potentially malignant cells. Her first thought was that she was dying. Her next thought was that she couldn't bear more children. She also realized that she'd have to be away from work, and her career was endangered as well, especially if people at her company learned of her problem.

After climbing the corporate ladder and giving the job everything she had, Carole wasn't happy. A ceiling blocked further progress, and she started to feel bored and burned out. She asked herself if she should look for a new job. Should she find a husband? Raise a family? She wondered if she had the energy for a major change. Her plan for her life didn't include this.

What began as a terrific marriage fell apart with no hope of saving it. Divorce wasn't part of the script Beth had for her life. She felt she'd failed and wondered if she'd ever have a meaningful relationship again. She had to rev up her career ambitions now too, but didn't feel very confident. She wondered how she'd make it financially, not to mention emotionally.

Allison had a new baby just as her career was really getting under way. She'd have loved spending more time at home, but didn't want to give up the professional standing she'd worked so hard to achieve. She was pulled in both directions. What would become of her career if she took a longer leave? How would she feel later if she missed some precious time with her baby?

These are the scenarios many women are confronting: We face opportunities, conflicts and choices we hadn't reckoned on.

In the beginning were our ambitions. Not our little-girl fantasies about being a ballerina or fire fighter, but those brave plans we made as women of a new era. Many of us wanted to be the best in our professions or in a specialty where we'd shown promise. We wanted fulfilling careers, solid marriages, very possibly motherhood and a gracious home as well.

Along came life, and our ambitions were postponed, modified or even ambushed!

In many instances, unforeseen forces beyond our control disrupted the smooth course we had mapped out so confidently. Sometimes those forces struck suddenly—a company takeover, death of someone close, illness. Sometimes too, they built gradually and were part of some major trend. Trends making headlines that seemed at first to have little impact on us as individuals often infiltrated even the most secure and settled lives. Mergers, takeovers and leveraged buyouts became very real to a talented graphic artist who'd never read the *Wall Street Journal* when her company was bought and her division eliminated.

It's hard enough to keep up with trends without having to anticipate them, cope with them and incorporate them in our future plans. But cope we must. Isolating ourselves from what's happening won't work. Ignoring our own wishes and desires can have a negative effect on our productivity in the long run too.

How can we realize our ambitions and get more of what we want in a fast-paced world with few guarantees, few certainties? These are times that call for a new way of looking at lives and careers. We need new coping skills and new strategies for initiating change. The more adept we are at initiating change, the more nearly our futures will match our expectations. First let's look at the process itself.

THE PROCESS OF CHANGE

Something happens and things are never the same. **Change occurs when things can't or don't continue as they were.** Things are shaken up, split apart, heaped together or replaced. They're transformed or pass from one phase to another—passages, if you will.

Change demands that we adjust and adapt. Our old attitudes and behaviors won't work anymore. We need time and resources to find new ones which do. The transition we undergo when change occurs, getting from "x" to "y," entails a series of steps or stages, moving forward, then backward, through a gamut of emotions.

Change invariably means letting go of something, and we experience this as a loss. Even if we initiate change ourselves—filing for divorce, moving to a new city—letting go of the past can be difficult. The new job may be a better fit, but saying good-bye to colleagues, moving out of the old office and forsaking the old routine can be wrenching. Women in the seventies and eighties reaching out for different slices of life, bearing the brunt of being tokens and venturing into new arenas, risked their security and often their marriages, as well as the possibility of professional failure. Many of these women experienced real losses as well as gains.

Getting fired, a divorce that you didn't see coming, a health crisis—these are called "trigger events" by counselors. When they're thrust upon you, they evoke a whole sequence of emotions.

The first is usually denial. Many people about to be terminated refuse to see "the handwriting on the wall." The "handwriting" may be as clear as the appearance of a new employee, the absence of new projects or a cold shoulder from the boss. Individuals ignore the symptoms of serious illness too. Yet it's perfectly natural: You want to believe everything is all right, you keep hoping things will improve, even when it's obvious they won't.

When you can no longer deny that something is happening, you may feel sad, depressed, betrayed, abandoned or even relieved. You may be on a roller coaster with a few highs amid the lows. Things start looking up briefly, then wham, you're dragged down again, lower than ever. You might develop symptoms of physical illness or become genuinely sick. This grim phase will pass, however. Mourning the things or people you leave behind can be a necessary phase that you must go through before you begin moving ahead.

Before long, you may get angry. You might blame someone in particular or simply the system. At this stage some people decide to write angry letters or even to sue the person or organization they believe has wronged them. Although acting on these impulses is usually not a good idea, anger itself is a healthy sign. It means you are willing to become actively involved again.

Whether you experience anger or not, eventually you summon up the energy to take some positive action. You may not know the direction of your new ambitions, but you see a glimmer of light at the end of the tunnel and keep moving toward it. You tap your coping abilities, plug into your network of colleagues, begin investigating alternatives and soon you're making things happen.

A LIFE-SPAN PERSPECTIVE

Experts once thought that adults were monolithic in their growth. Supposedly, we grew up, became adults, lived our lives and then died, with really very little change. Experts now acknowledge a series of crises or major transitions. **People are almost certain to undergo role changes as they experience life events or "triggers" that alter how they view themselves and others.**

These events may differ greatly, yet they fall into patterns and themes with similarities. **As they pile up over time, these events season us, giving us wisdom and maturity. They sharpen our perceptions, help us hone our coping skills and enrich our resources.**

Early adult development research on white middle-class males had concluded that *all* adults experienced certain conflicts at certain *ages* and *stages* and faced certain life tasks to be mastered at specific times. Life supposedly had a *predictable* structure, with alternating fifteen-year periods of stability and shorter periods of instability and change. Women's lives were assumed to have a similar structure.

In the eighties women psychologists and doctoral candidates began testing these theories and finding, as I did, that they don't fit working women. Very possibly, they won't fit the latest generation of men, whose priorities and career patterns are shifting too.

A decade ago, everyone talked about the "mid-life crisis." It inspired cartoons, sit-com jokes and probably more than a few real-life rebellions as well. However, a closer look reveals that individuals of *all* ages undergo upheavals of their beliefs and goals. People from twenty to sixty and older change careers, start new relationships, adopt different life-styles and even face their mortality. **We're all in the same boat on the same turbulent sea regardless of age.**

Fewer and fewer careers remain stable for fifteen years, as was once thought. Sadly too, many relationships lack the durability they once seemed to have. Even if you have stayed in a certain career or in a relationship for fifteen years, you're likely to have undergone other major changes. The fifteen-year cycle seems to be the product of a slower, more tranquil time or a simpler view of life.

Sometimes I ask people in groups: Do you know anyone among your friends with *all* areas of their life (career, relations, self-development, life-style, health) "together" or settled to their liking? Almost no one can name more than a person or two. Stability is shorter these days, instability more frequent and unpredictable.

We bring on change in this fast-changing world too. We're socialized to look ahead and to strive constantly to earn more, do better, achieve greater status. **We keep setting greater expectations for ourselves, and may feel guilty at getting stuck on a plateau or heading downhill.** Those who drop out of the race usually find some new game or goal to pursue. Any educated American (or anyone Americanized) in this day and age probably won't be idle for long.

All of us, men and women, are far from static, finished products as once was thought. Although we may carry certain character traits with us for our lifetimes, we also have wide margins for growth. We can gain independence, new skills, self-esteem and more sophisticated styles of coping.

MAJOR CHANGES IN WOMEN'S LIVES

If you're a woman alive and working, you've probably experienced some major life changes as these five women have. **Whether you realized it or not at the time, the discoveries and choices you made as you coped helped shape the major themes and ambitions in your life.**

Sometimes we learn more easily by unraveling the themes and discerning the patterns in other people's lives. Allison, Beth, Carole, Diana and Elinor (note the alphabetical order to help you remember their names) are probably like women you already know. For now, we'll look at each in just one crisis.

As you read about these women, note the variety of their responses and see if you identify with one more than with the others. While their careers may be different from yours, their issues will sound familiar. Seeing their responses to change can help you understand and improve your *own* responses and coping mechanisms.

Allison's Work/Family Conflict

When I met Allison Franklin in 1989, she was forty-five, a senior attorney for a *Fortune* 100 energy company. A tall, striking blonde, meticulously groomed, she wore horn-rimmed glasses that were serious looking though flattering in the way they enlarged her blue-gray eyes. A New Englander, she seemed almost aloof, yet she had a nervous manner. She shrugged the broad shoulders of her crisp gray suit to emphasize a point.

We met in her walnut-paneled, book-lined office overlooking the city's downtown skyline. The room was so quiet I wanted to whisper.

She asked to have her calls held and closed the door to her office. "I think of life as a series of challenges, really." She spoke in a precise way, tapping her nails against the desk. "You have setbacks, you meet them. You accept your responsibilities too. Where emotions are concerned, well, you try not to let them get in the way."

I asked then about the career-family conflict she'd had.

Her oval face softened as she began to speak. "That was a tough one. The real conflict was with my second baby, not my first."

When her first child, Kathy, was born, Allison already had a degree in biochemistry. Discouraged about opportunities for women in the sciences, she switched to paralegal work and was studying law at night. "I quit the paralegal job, and in that six months, finished up my law degree. When I went back to work, I joined this company as an administrative assistant. We had a wonderful housekeeper, Mattie, during those years.

"Scotty was born when Kathy was four and I was associate counsel by then. Scotty wasn't the problem. I was. I didn't want to leave him. Those little hands grab yours, and those wonderful blue eyes gaze at you so trusting. . . . Mom became a mushy lawyer around him.

"I had worked so hard—night school, paralegal work, all those damn contracts for service stations. After paying my dues, was I going to give it up and begin back at the beginning? What would my boss and colleagues say? 'We told you so—another dropout woman'?"

She shook her head. "Besides, we needed the money. My husband's family and my family had helped us buy the house in Teaneck. I didn't like taking the money, but we were going to pay back every cent. I'd planned to go right back to work, and suddenly I wanted to be home with Scotty instead. I didn't know I'd feel that way."

There weren't as many professional women then, and far fewer of them having babies. Women today hear from friends and colleagues about how they felt torn when it came time to return to work. Many echo Allison's words—"I didn't know I'd feel that way!" Motherhood is a change that brings on new emotions, even a new identity. For once in Allison's life, she had no logical response to a challenge confronting her.

Beth Faces Divorce

Elizabeth Gregson, known as Beth to her friends, was fifty-one at the time of our interview. Director of technical training at a major insurance company, she was dressed in a tweed suit that, along with her naturally graying brown hair, made her look more like the professor she had been in an earlier career. She leaned back in an ergonomic chair, talking on the phone, as the receptionist ushered me into her office. She smiled and quickly drew her conversation to a close with, "Say hello to all the relatives. Bye for now."

Her "Bye" sounded more like "Bah." I commented on the hint of a Southern accent.

"That was my mother on the phone just now. Yes, I'm from the South, Virginia. I tried hard to keep it from showing when I first got to New York.

Didn't want to seem like a Southern belle, but it just slips out again when I'm talking with kin."

The accent faded as she spoke knowledgeably about the changes technology had made in her new field. After she showed me her training setup with its computer consoles, satellite hookups and interactive video segments, I asked her to tell me about a major crisis of her life.

"I was an assistant professor when I met my husband-to-be. He was charming and funny, more outgoing than I am, and quite a catch. We were both teaching in Roanoke and went out a lot with a small circle of friends. We entertained too. It was a nice, cozy life for almost five years. No children—we thought we had time.

"Then we didn't get tenure, neither of us. I realized they'd never tenure a woman. My chairman was so unenlightened. He couldn't see women as full professors or colleagues. I'd been so naive. I hadn't realized how few women were tenured professors. For some other women who taught college, not getting tenure was a signal that it was time to stay home and have babies." She clasped her hands together as she talked.

"In my ex-husband's case, his college insisted he publish. He didn't. That's when it all fell apart. He became depressed, started drinking, even hit me. It was disgusting. How could I have married such a loser? I'd had an alcoholic father, and my husband was becoming like him." Her body tensed up as she spoke.

"I don't like to think about it. I tried to cover for him and carry the load for both of us. But in a small town, *everybody* knows your business.

"I felt like the heroine in some Southern gothic novel. There I was, trapped in Virginia, worrying about my survival but embarrassed to tears, lest anyone figure out what was happening—my marriage a disaster, my career cut short. I had to escape my alcoholic husband, of course. Then I had to take stock of my abilities and find somewhere else I could make a living. For a while I wondered if I'd ever get my life in control again."

For Beth more than for most people, exercising control over herself and her environment was important. She was also a person who saw life as a series of choices or forks in the road with decisions to be made at each. There were roads not taken too, perhaps with a twinge of regret for "might-have-beens." At the time of her divorce, she saw herself as a failure and blamed herself for the choices she had made, as if there were only one "right" set of options. Even in this crisis, though, Beth found some new options.

Carole Fights Burnout

Carole Hawks at thirty-three had risen to be a marketing vice president at one of New York's top ten banks. A solid, handsome woman with skin the color of teak, she'd had to cope with being a minority as well as being female in what is still very much a white man's world.

Over the years since our first interview, her hair and fashions had changed, as her smooth professional image evolved. She had become more regal with time, and on this day wore a soft peach and beige ensemble with chunky African jewelry.

We met at noon at a lunch spot known to have the best chili around. "My life's a series of doors," she told me when I asked how she saw her history to date. "I keep knocking and opportunities arise or I stir them up. Some doors are easier to open than others. I try to stay on my toes, anticipating what might happen next!"

One of the first minorities mentored and promoted in her bank, Carole had gained skills in marketing bank services. She moved from coordinating corporate-sponsored, citywide athletic events to consumer surveys of branch services and on to her present position, managing the next generation of credit cards with thousands of bits of personal information about a consumer stored on a computer chip.

She now had a staff charged with the detail work she once performed. Her salary was impressive too—about three times the top amount her father earned. But things weren't nearly as perfect as they seemed.

"I don't know if I can take it much longer," she said, shaking her head. "I feel burned out. Our bank has a revolving door. You no sooner figure out what makes one boss tick, than you've got another one who wants something else. The one I have now is the pits. Unreasonable. Doesn't know what she wants. Always looks for somebody else to blame. The stress is catching up with me."

This wasn't the only area of Carole's life bothering her. Not long before, her mother had died and she'd gone back to Chicago to take care of funeral arrangements. Then she and her live-in boyfriend, Malcolm, had broken up and there was no chance of getting back together.

"I feel the clock is ticking and I'm back to square one. Opportunity, please knock—now—while this girl can still answer." She heaved a weary sigh. I had never seen Carole, normally a take-charge kind of woman, the kind nobody messes with, so subdued.

"Maybe I'm in mourning. Maybe it will pass. All I know is it's sure an effort to pull myself together every morning. At least I've *got* a job. Some of my friends have been looking for months. This competition's fierce. I can't let up now. . . ." She pushed her half-eaten chili aside. After being a token and overcoming discrimination and sexual harassment to get this far, Carole, like so many other women, ended up asking, "Is that all there is?"

"Maybe I should have a baby? No, that's crazy. What's happened to my plans? I'm not supposed to feel like this. I should be grateful for my successes. I wish it weren't so hard. You'd better stay tuned so I don't self-destruct." She eased out of the booth, a troubled look on her striking, classic face.

For once Carole couldn't see opportunities or a doorway out of her doldrums. Carole had anticipated a steady upward path in her career. Not only did she have to deal with the loss of two of her most significant relationships, but the lack of satisfaction in her job had zapped her career enthusiasm. In the past, Carole had responded to difficulties with "No problem," but now things were ganging up on her. It happens to the best of women.

She had coped well until now, however, always trying new angles. We'll find out a little later how she handled this crisis.

Diana Feels She's Dying

Diana Ramirez Issacs, thirty-eight, was a stocky, warm woman with shiny black cropped hair. Every time we met, she wore a wide friendly smile and would try to turn the interview around to talk about me. Diana liked people and it showed.

Originally from California, with a Hispanic background, she became a communications manager at a multinational cosmetics and personal-care products company. There she gained experience editing newsletters, annual reports, company magazines and brochures, as well as writing speeches for the company's top officers. At the time of this meeting, she was the mother of two, Jason and Kimmy, and lived on a quiet street in the Park Slope section of Brooklyn in an old Victorian house with her devoted husband, Nate.

We sat at the round table in her silver, black and red office at her company's midtown headquarters tower. Artwork and wall hangings from her earlier life softened the high-tech edges of her company's decor. Her nubby red jacket dress went well with the setting.

"I imagine my life as a story, a saga, as though I'm writing my own chapters in a novel. Some chapters have been easier to write than others," she told me.

"The roughest part in my saga, so far, happened when we were hoping to have a second child. I'd had a miscarriage the previous year, but I'd always been healthy like my mother. I was thirty-four. After my regular checkup, the gynecologist had me come back. The Pap smear showed precancerous cells and he recommended a hysterectomy.

"All I heard was cancer. I'll never forget it. I thought, 'This can't be me. He's made a mistake!' I burst into tears without hearing the rest. I went home to Park Slope in a cab, something I rarely do, and kept sobbing to the driver about dying so young, leaving my son, never having any more children if I did live.

"Once I was home, I called a woman friend who listened and empathized and told me it probably wasn't as bad as all that. She also pointed out something I'd almost forgotten—that I'd better not let anybody at work find out. The big 'C' could be the *unofficial* reason for firing perfectly competent people!

"I hope I never go through anything like that again. Not only was I scared for my life, I was really cut off from the support I needed. My family is on the West Coast, and many of my women friends were work colleagues I didn't dare tell! Nate was wonderful, though. He understood and listened even when I'd say crazy things."

Diana had assumed that, like her parents, she'd be healthy until her sixties, seventies or beyond. At any age we tell ourselves, we're too young for a serious or life-threatening illness. We may be so confident that we neglect to have adequate health insurance and emergency funds to cope with such a crisis. Yet any of us can have a health emergency. Diana had insurance, fortunately, but other less tangible phases of her crisis demanded some complex coping skills, as we'll see later.

Elinor Gets Fired

Elinor Jacoby was just twenty-eight, a vivacious, auburn-haired accessory buyer at a second tier buying office. She draped her tiny frame in layers of black, dotted with bright, hand-painted jewelry. Her outfit concealed her thinness.

She waved away a cloud of smoke as I entered her cramped closet of an office. There was barely room for the two of us. She whisked a messy pile of papers and jewelry boxes from a stool so I could sit to take notes.

"My life's pretty chaotic by most people's standards," Elinor said. "My career has been so checkered, so full of surprises, which I don't always love—like the one that floored me a few seasons ago. That was the pits. I just wanted to end it. I felt so desperate."

Elinor was a New Yorker born and bred, she'd told me when we first met, as if her distinct Long Island accent didn't give it away. As she grimaced, a slightly crooked front tooth added character. If her office space had been larger, I was sure she'd have been pacing. She was conscious of her image, yet unable to sit still.

"I was so proud of myself, making it on my own without my family. My parents had retired in Florida and my brother was in Seattle. I was paying my dues, working on the training squad at a department store and got promoted to assistant buyer for costume jewelry. I loved shopping the market with my boss. I was doing well, I thought. So I didn't complain when they transferred me to New Haven to do my stint at a branch. It was the boonies, but a necessary step in becoming a buyer. They'd almost promised me a slot at my review.

"But I felt like I was doing time in New Haven—on my feet all day and no social life, none! Then boom! The store ran low on money, sold out to a British conglomerate that couldn't bail them out and people like me got axed!" Her hand slashed her throat like an imaginary machete.

"There I was. Stuck in New Haven with no money, no friends, no prospects. How was I to move back to New York, keep my creditors at bay, look for work and not make another mistake? It was very chaotic. Of course, I was out of touch with everyone, even my markets. Arrrrghhhh! I was really furious at what they'd done to me and mad at myself too for trusting them. You can't always see what companies are up to! You'd have to have a crystal ball!"

Like many people in crisis, Elinor lashed out this way and that and at herself. "Why didn't I see what was happening? How could they/he/she do this to me?" When she wasn't angry, Elinor felt overwhelmed at having to deal with so many things at once: getting a loan from somewhere, moving to where the opportunities were, getting back in touch with her contacts, finding a new job with promise. She knew that some aspects of her crisis such as losing touch with colleagues and not saving money for such an emergency were her own doing.

In a situation such as Elinor's when things seem to be falling apart around us, if we lay all the blame on outside forces, we're fooling ourselves. And worse, we're missing a chance to learn from the experience.

You've no doubt noted each woman had a different type of crisis. Perhaps you're also aware that each perceived her crisis, her choices and, in fact, her life differently too.

TYPES OF CHANGES—THEMES AND PATTERNS IN OUR LIVES

In my research and counseling, I've questioned hundreds of professional women about the major changes in their lives and careers, asking them to describe whatever changes were important to them. These categories emerged:

1. Career Changes
2. Personal Lives: Role and Relationship Changes
3. Self-Developmental Challenges
4. Life-Style Changes
5. Health Changes

Career Changes

Fifty percent of major life changes working women described to me relate to careers.

Let go while stranded at the company's New Haven branch, Elinor blamed herself for her plight—out of work, out of money and away from the opportunities in her field. She'd made some errors in judgment and she knew what they were.

More and more women professionals have been in her shoes. If not fired, they've been disappointed by developments—or lack of them—in their careers. Perhaps the raise, promotion or partnership doesn't come. Typically, we blame ourselves, doubting our abilities or questioning our original ambitions. Men are more likely to blame the situation, the merger or takeover or cutback, or the company at which their merits were not sufficiently appreciated. Men's interpretations of a firing may be less candid, yet it enables them to get back on their feet. Women's attitudes help them learn from their experiences if they don't go overboard in self-recrimination or doubts about themselves.

It's not too unusual for women to go to extremes, however. Maybe even you or someone you know has jumped to a new career or dropped out of the work force to be a full-time homemaker or mother after a major career letdown. In such a move, a woman seems to be saying, "If I can't win at this game, I'll try a different game." Men usually don't have the option of forsaking the game they're in.

Carole faced burnout after many successful moves that whetted her appetite for the pay and perks that go with a high-status bank job.

It's a rare career these days that advances without setbacks, but the career paths of women in particular are anything but smooth. By 1988, only five in a group of forty-five women I started tracking in 1978 were working for the same company, and of these five, four were talking of leaving, some for entirely different careers. The message is unmistakable: Women are voting with their feet, moving on in new career directions. We'll look at new ways of shaping your career later on.

Personal Lives:
Role and Relationship Changes

In my research, twenty-four percent of the major changes in women's lives came from the area of personal roles and relationship changes. These changes involved families, friends and intimate relationships. Women described events such as marriage, the birth of a child, children leaving home and children getting into trouble. They mentioned separation from parents, divorce, the breakup of long-term relationships. They also listed the death of a parent, husband, child or friend. **None of these events leave us untouched, though some have greater impact than others.** Some alter our roles irrevocably. Carole, when there was no one else to plan her mother's funeral, rose to the occasion. However, when parents die, we experience not only the loss of loved ones, but the loss of the role we've played the longest. We are no longer children, but suddenly promoted to an older generation with new roles and responsibilities. The death of parents is also an unwelcome reminder of our own mortality, a realization that can have a powerful impact on our ambitions.

There's really no dress rehearsal for becoming a mother, ceasing to be a daughter or becoming a widow. Learning how others handled these major passages can broaden your understanding, however. So can being a listener or giving whatever help you can when friends come to these crossroads, whether they're new mothers or new widows or are saying good-bye to one of their dreams. We'll look at the impact of events such as these in more depth later.

Self-Developmental Challenges

Ours may be the first generation to live our "past lives" during this one. How often do we hear people say, "I was 'X' in a former life" while meaning a previous phase or career?

There's a rebirth of the Renaissance person. Perhaps it's in a view of life, if not as a banquet, then as a smorgasbord with many choices.

In my research and counseling groups, I've observed that women's education was often not related or not relevant to their present careers or the new directions they'd chosen. They were also generally more highly educated than their male colleagues.

I've asked these women about their reasons for continuing their education. What is noteworthy is that their efforts to improve themselves, discover and develop their potential were deliberate and voluntary. Although employers frequently require continuing education, rarely had anyone prodded these women to learn. They had made up their own minds to become more skilled, more educated, better in some way.

More often than men, women feel a deficit, a dissatisfaction with what they are or can do or how little they know. They may be more cautious than men in wanting to know all they can before making a next move, whether it's a career move or decorating an apartment.

Instead of dwelling on our imperfections, we need to focus on our strengths and our potential. A slightly overweight woman might find that a public speaking class would serve her confidence better than a weight-loss programs. It's time we stop trying to fix what isn't broken.

If we choose carefully among the many options we have for enhancing who we are and what we know, these efforts can alter our ambitions in many positive ways.

Life-style Changes

This is the most difficult to define of all the categories. It includes relocation and culture changes as well. Often this type of change goes hand in hand with job changes, yet women listed it separately. Perhaps women are more conscious of life-style differences.

Women I spoke with described geographical relocations: moving from East to West, North to South, and vice versa, or from rural to suburban or to small towns or leaving their parents' homes for places of their own. After failing to get tenure at her university and leaving her alcoholic husband, Beth made a life-style change too, in moving to New York.

While some women might have retreated to a familiar setting, Beth wanted to turn over her new leaf and put the unpleasantness of the past behind her. With her historian's outlook, Beth was sensitive to the many differences that make up a "sense of place."

Elinor was the most traveled of our five, with buying trips to China, Hong Kong, Taiwan, Korea, India, all over Europe and parts of South America too. She was extremely aware of certain aspects of a culture, but not of others. She knew the native arts and crafts that formed the basis for the unusual accessories she sought out. She could tell you how a Peruvian belt was made. She also tried to keep abreast of factors that affected manufacturing costs and accessibility of raw materials.

Her intellectual curiosity was pinpointed on those few things. Her linguistic abilities were minimal. She was unaware of South America's leading novelists or of social and political problems outside the United States unless a strike threatened.

Elinor's ability to screen out some things, focusing on others, made her extremely effective in her chosen career. Being aware of the variety of our experiences, the subtle and not-so-subtle differences, can add richness and resilience to our lives.

Health Changes

Sooner or later, health becomes a life or death matter. We tenaciously avoid thinking about health issues. We assume we'll be healthy forever, and may ignore warning signs of disease. Caught in a health crisis, we may confide in the people closest to us, but become secretive with others, especially work colleagues. Among the illnesses professional women tend to keep under wraps are arthritis, lupus, PMS and cancer. Companies, especially those trying to cut health-care costs, can be reluctant to hire a person who has cancer. Women are especially secretive about conditions specific to females. A woman being treated for PMS said, "I wouldn't want to provide men who are skeptical of women with more ammunition to do us in!"

Research on men emphasizes the trauma of heart attacks. Women with cancer, however, seem better able to cope. Having nurtured children, co-workers, spouses and others perhaps strengthens our inner resources. Possibly too, our nurturing capacities cause us to think of others even when facing a personal crisis of our own. **Any life-threatening illness— our own or that of someone close to us—makes us stop and ask,**

"What am I doing with my life?" Awareness of mortality forces us to rethink our ambitions.

Perhaps you haven't been accustomed to compartmentalizing your life into five areas as I've done here. In real life, the different areas flow into each other, mingle and overlap in myriad ways. Categories are essential to research, of course, and they can also be useful to you in navigating your way through a crisis. If an upheaval occurs in one part of your life, say the career area, but things are fine in all other areas, you probably feel you can weather the storm. When things begin to go wrong in three or four areas, your life becomes more tumultuous and difficult. We all need at least one safe harbor from the storm, one place we can fall back on, feel good about, where there are resources for us to tap. Compartmentalizing your life in this way can sometimes lead you to an area of safety with a wealth of resources you might otherwise overlook. Some individuals are more adept at this than others, as we'll see.

Now let's take a closer look at the major changes in *your* life. The following exercise will help you see where you've been, so you'll discover important links between your past and the future you want.

EXERCISE I

YOUR MAJOR LIFE CHANGES—YOU'VE COPED BEFORE!

(1) What major changes have you experienced since age twenty-nine? Or since college or age eighteen? This checklist covers many of the changes adults experience over time. **Your storehouse of experiences helps make you the person you are and can help you prepare for the future too.**

YOUR LIFE EXPERIENCES CHECKLIST

Just circle any words or phrases that represent life experiences or changes you've been through. There are blanks in each category to add others. This takes about ten minutes.

Your Career

1. Started a new job or career.
2. Changed jobs or careers.
3. Dealt with difficult bosses and work situations.

4. Learned from a mentor.
5. Been fired.
6. Been promoted.
7. Become a boss.
8. Achieved greater autonomy, more freedom to do it your way.
9. Invested in, reassessed your skills and career.
10. Integrated your career into your life.
11. Been passed over, not promoted.
12. Become a mentor, role model, coach for those who are younger.
13. Come to terms with work versus family conflicts.
14. Shifted emphasis from advancement at work to productivity or challenging projects.
15. Coasted at work while other areas of your life took over.
16. Gained more seniority in your profession.
17. Become the oldest person where you work.
18. Been plateaued, offtrack, stalled in your career.

19. _____

20. _____

Now, before moving to the next section, star (*) the key events that have changed your life the most.

Your Relationships/Roles

1. Outgrown your expectations of what's "appropriate" adult behavior.
2. Survived in spite of losses and deaths.
3. Integrated role changes as your parents aged, the children in your life grew up.
4. Developed closer attachments to others, deepened friendships.
5. Needed and used support systems.
6. Ended relationships.
7. Become a parent, taken care of others.
8. Faced an empty nest.
9. Dealt with family death, family illness, divorce.
10. Had role conflicts or role changes.
11. Been married or widowed.

12. _____

13. _____

Now star (*) the key relationship changes that altered your life.

Your Self-Development

1. Integrated previously neglected parts of your personality (creativity/feelings, etc.).
2. Developed personal internal standards—no longer living based on the expectations of others.
3. Become competitive, confident, self-directed, mature, less tied to your parents.
4. Become more tolerant of yourself and others.
5. Appreciated the complexity of yourself and others.
6. Made a concerted effort to change your behavior, attitudes, perceptions.
7. Accepted imperfections in yourself and others.
8. Come to terms with contradictory parts of yourself (risk taking/playing it safe, etc.).
9. Realized that life is not simple, fair or controllable and that there is evil in the world.
10. Integrated the masculine/feminine polarities in yourself.
11. Acquired wisdom and a new perspective on things.
12. Decreased your anxiety and loneliness.
13. Dealt with dependence, independence and interdependence.
14. Valued personal growth within a career.
15. Been powerful, dominant, assertive.
16. Changed your self-concept, who you are. Becoming more of "a," less of "b."
17. Shifted from what others think is important to what you think is important.

18. _____

19. _____

Now star (*) any key items on this list that changed your life significantly.

Your Life-Style

1. Seen your life in the context of history and events, realized how you're affected by them.
2. Reassessed your life-style, status, relationships, career, taken stock of who you are and what's important to you.
3. Shifted your view of the future.
4. Come to terms with your dreams versus reality.
5. Closed one chapter of your life, begun another.
6. Had a radical change in your work or home environment.

7. Moved from one sector of the economy to another (profit to not-for-profit, business to government to education, etc.).
8. Moved from one area of the United States to another or abroad.
9. Settled into a comfortable routine.
10. Balanced demands of self, family, career.
11. Been financially secure or insecure.

12. _____

13. _____

Now star (*) your top life-style changes, the ones with the most impact on you.

Your Health

1. Come to terms with eventual death and bodily decline in yourself and others.
2. Become aware of your health and aging.
3. Had a sense of poor health, been unhappy about it.
4. Had a sense of well-being in spite of growing older or having an illness.
5. Had major surgery or a major or chronic illness.
6. Decided whether to have children or not, given your biological clock.
7. Given birth to a child.
8. Dealt with infertility.
9. Made a major, sustained effort through exercise, diet, stress reduction to improve your health and/or appearance.
10. Changed your perspective regarding the time you have yet to live.

11. _____

12. _____

Now star (*) any key health events that have changed your life.

Note: These items and those in Exercise II are ones cited by my interviewees, students and counselees, and build on the work of Drs. Roger Gould, Daniel Levinson, Nancy Schlossberg, Susan Kintner, Douglas Hall, Donald Super, Malcolm Knowles, Carol Gilligan and others who've researched the lives of adults.

(2) Now look at all the items you've circled in each category. Count them. Isn't it amazing how much you've experienced over time?

(3) How are you different now? Perhaps stronger, wiser, more mature?____

DOMINO AND DISCRETE CHANGES

As you've surely observed from your experience or from the five women's crises described earlier in this chapter, individuals are very different in the way they respond to a crisis. Some people seem to fall apart, while others simply take life's trials in stride. But it's more complex than that; in fact, this difference leads to the coping styles I'll introduce in the next chapter.

When I analyzed my interviews, I noticed that some changes women described were more complex and tumultuous. For some lives, the cliche "It never rains but it pours" really fits. Some individuals describe a whole deluge of different events occurring all at once. One thing seems to trigger another.

A divorce might be followed by a move to a new city, a new career and a new identity. An illness might set off a chain of events that include problems in close relationships as well as at work. Carole's job burnout, loss of her mother and breakup with her boyfriend caused her to call her whole existence into question. Elinor's firing coincided with financial problems, her lack of a professional network and the realization that she'd lost many friends and colleagues to AIDS.

I call this clustering of events Domino changes. Things fall like dominoes. What is important here isn't just the way events pile up one on top of another, however, but the fact that the individuals *perceive* them as happening this way. One woman said, "Everything was happening all at once. I thought I was drowning!" The events might be totally unrelated, but these women found connections and linkages. Recalling such an experience later, one woman said: "That was the spring everything went wrong. My husband nearly died, my boss got fired and I broke my ankle! I think the message was that I should take things easier, not be so hard on myself."

The "message," she said, as though some greater meaning could be found. The women who describe these Domino clusters typically ponder large, hard-to-answer questions such as "Why me?" or "What does it all mean?" "Why is all this happening to me?" is one that seems to imply that the cruel hand of fate is at work. Yes, some women in Domino episodes feel victimized, as Elinor did. On the other hand, "What is the meaning of all this?" is a question that implies that there's something to be learned from the experience, no matter how terrible or turbulent. We'll look into the potential for learning from these episodes as we go along.

One after another, professional women told me about these experiences. Usually dressed in business attire, crisp and efficient, they stepped out of character as the emotions—pain, sadness or anger—resurfaced in the telling. If you've ever been through a Domino change, you know how it feels. There's no mistaking one once you're in the middle of it. When I tell audiences about Domino changes, people who've had them nod in recognition. Others, however, are more critical and need convincing.

Not everybody experiences Domino changes.

As I found in my research, sometimes to my surprise, other professional women described events just as momentous—the death of a child or a divorce—in a matter-of-fact manner without emotions. "This happened, then this . . ." Even when they'd undergone a series of difficulties within a short period of time, they described the events one by one without an attempt to make connections between them. Totally calm, they seemed to be reciting a checklist!

The absence of emotions was what struck me at first. Instead of revealing their feelings, they categorized their life events in an almost scientific way, drawing clear lines between their personal and professional lives. They spoke with pride about the steps and the strategies they'd taken. They also seemed to have coped more easily, without being overwhelmed or victimized, and without probing for underlying meanings.

To make some sense of the differences, I drew what I call a Change Continuum and began to array the women's names along it. At the left were those who described their life events one at a time, gave less evidence of emotion and seemed to cope more easily. I labeled these changes Discrete.

At the opposite end were those who described similar events as occurring in a cluster, one on top of another, overlapping and interrelated. These women let their emotions show and had seemingly had a harder time handling it all. These were the women whose lives were marked by Domino changes.

Two somewhat surprising discoveries were soon apparent. One was that the names along the Change Continuum had a gap in the middle. Most women either had one type of experience or they had the other. None had an equal number of both types of change. All of us, of course, have occasional Discrete events, but some individuals live their entire lives without once undergoing tumultuous Domino changes.

The other discovery came later. Upon investigating the lives of the women in more depth, I confirmed what I'd suspected earlier—the women with Domino events were more spontaneous and more creative in their response to different changes, even simple, one-at-a-time events. They were more easily thrown for a loop, yet they took bigger risks, seemingly inviting more turmoil. **Not only did the two groups perceive these happenings differently, which made an enormous difference, they thought and behaved differently too. Their perception of the world and their whole way of dealing with it was different.**

Both groups had positive role gains, to be sure. Both had become wives, mothers, executives. Both had an equal number of voluntary and involuntary changes. But the women at the Domino end cited more role losses: divorces and other instances of leaving behind an old life for a new one.

I didn't stop investigating this topic after my dissertation was published in 1985, but went on asking, "Why this difference in the way women experience change?" Interviewing the same women who had been near the Discrete end of the Continuum in 1988, I found some had undergone job losses yet were still matter-of-fact and controlled in their responses. Those who were near the Domino end were still emotional. When an event called for enthusiasm, they showed it too.

Other research cites differences in how men live with change. Like the blind men feeling the elephant, we're all trying to describe what we have here. Daniel Levinson in *Seasons of a Man's Life* noted that some men have tumultuous changes while others do not. Paula Robbins in *Successful Midlife Career Change* found similar differences among ninety-one men. I wondered about the lives of contemporary professional women, who must undergo many changes in order to function in their careers. Why aren't we more alike in the way we experience many of the same events?

Other types of research may help clarify what's happening here. For some years now, we've labeled people left-brained and right-brained. The left-brained are more analytical, critical and controlled, like the women near the Discrete end of the spectrum. The right-brained are more emotional, risk-taking and creative, as I found those near the Domino end were. We learned next that genetics and biochemical makeup may lie behind certain behavioral differences. One chemical affects risk-taking, thrill and stimulation-seeking behavior observed in those near the Domino end. With differing amounts of certain chemicals, a person may strive to remain in control, want to play it safe and be harder to arouse, like the individuals at the Discrete end. Perhaps there are genes and molecules at play here.

Numerous psychologists and behavioral scientists have described personality types. The Myers-Briggs Type Indicator with its sixteen personality types, based on C. G. Jung's theories of personality, is widely used today. It would identify the people with Discrete changes as thinking, judging and sensing, and those with Domino events as intuitive, perceiving and feeling.

Recent research on personality traits concludes that an individual's anxiety level, friendliness and eagerness for novel experiences change little throughout life. My hunch is that an individual's position on the Change Continuum stays much the same too, although our experiences—especially professional women's experiences—alter our coping styles, as we'll see shortly.

Meanwhile, in a Domino world, perceiving events as more Discrete pieces of the whole can help you regain some control and be less whiplashed by emotions. Not every crisis breaks down easily into Discrete events, however. Nor should you avoid the soul-searching a Domino crisis can evoke. As you might have guessed by now, the best place to be is close to the middle ground. You'll learn techniques to help you cope, no matter where you place yourself on the Continuum.

DISCRETES, DOMINOES AND CAREERS

Research on seventy-five high-level women at The Center for Creative Leadership concluded what many of us have believed for some time—that women must walk a tightrope to survive and succeed in careers. Only certain behaviors are acceptable for women in corporations.

If you've "been there," you know what it's like. You don't dare appear too masculine or too feminine, too aggressive or too nurturing. You choose your clothing with considerable care, nothing too frilly but certainly nothing mannish; perhaps you soften your pinstripes with silk. You also limit your vocabulary and even the things you talk about. Yes, you should know about yesterday's football game, but maybe you'd better keep your opinion on the president's speech to yourself, especially if your opinion is an unpopular one. It's okay to laugh at some jokes but look askance at others. You're always on guard, always calculating your risks. Some of you get used to this and some of you don't.

So it's not surprising that women at the Discrete end of the Continuum have survived longer in corporate careers. Less imaginative and less spontaneous, but more controlled and predictable, they've altered their behavior to mirror the culture of their companies. During periods of change, their sources of support were bosses, mentors and work colleagues. Women at the Domino end, however, saw people at work, particularly the boss, as "the enemy."

You're probably figuring out where you and people you know belong on the Continuum. Possibly you've already zeroed in on some of our five women. Allison, our coolly sophisticated lawyer, and Beth, our somewhat conservative training specialist, fall at the Discrete end. Consider Allison at an energy company and Beth at an insurance company. Both have played it safe, not rocking the boat. Ask them about their employers and they'd reply with positive comments, even if they felt differently. Both saw themselves as lucky to have reached the levels where they were, although Allison had her law degree and Beth, her Ph.D.

In conversations Allison and Beth got to the point quickly, without emotion. "No problem" was one of their favorite expressions. Looking back at potentially traumatic life events, they saw them as challenges or turning points. But they quickly got their lives under control.

You've probably noticed how people who stay in a career a long time begin to fit the stereotype for that career. Get on an elevator in a large office building and you'll see people who look and talk much alike exiting at the same floors. The tasks you perform and the people around you help mold you to conform to that environment. Not only each industry but each company and each department within a company has its own language, norms, procedures and unwritten rules. People at the Discrete end have little difficulty in conforming to what's expected of them in their jobs.

I found that women at the Domino end left large organizations sooner, having found less of a "fit." They hadn't found corporations supportive. They needed more autonomy, independence and creativity than large bureaucratic structures allow. Risk takers in most aspects of their lives, they were more likely to launch their own businesses. More open about their problems and private lives, they were more likely to have used therapy. In general, they'd undergone more role changes too.

Diana, the artist turned communications specialist, and Elinor, the retailing maverick, were close to the Domino end of the Continuum. One was caught in a health emergency, the other in a job crunch. Their emotions took over in a crisis if not before. They found most corporate cultures boring, liked to bend the rules and take chances. They were apt to be more creative and colorful in their dress too. Fortunately for Elinor, her field rewarded her creative flair.

Carole was closer to the middle of the Change Continuum but is on the Domino side. She had a chameleonlike ability to blend in wherever she was. She learned to play the game at her bank, where she was precise and efficient, but she hadn't shut out her emotions or extinguished her ability to take risks. Even coping with adversity, however, didn't make her immune to burnout.

Where do you see yourself on the Change Continuum? Place an x there. If you work for a large, traditional corporation, you've probably altered your behavior to fit in.

THE CHANGE CONTINUUM

DISCRETE |_____|_____| DOMINO
   Allison   Beth   Carole   Diana   Elinor

You've seen the differences exhibited by these five women. These next two exercises are designed to help you see how you typically respond to change.

EXERCISE II

YOUR PLACE ON THE CHANGE CONTINUUM

Select one of the key life changes you've starred on your checklist in Exercise I earlier in this chapter. **Knowing how you perceived this change will give you insight into your coping style.**

Put an "x" on the continuum below next to the words that best describe that change. Was your first change voluntary or involuntary, etc.? Now select a second change to score, and then a third, etc.

DISCRETE			DOMINO
Voluntary Change			Involuntary
Easy Change			Difficult
Role Gains			Losses
One Event			Multiple
Stand Alone			Interacting
Events			Events

Total x's _____   _____   _____

Where do most of your x's fall? Do you think you'd be more comfortable with Allison, Beth, Carole, Diana or Elinor? Who seems closest to you in her way of responding? How does this compare to your first x on the Change Continuum on the previous page? Now let's look at how you respond to change:

EXERCISE III

YOUR RESPONSE TO CHANGE

When you coped with these life events, how did you respond to change? Place an "x" on each line for each event, next to the word most like you. You will end up with four or five "x's" per line.

DISCRETE |_____|_____| DOMINO

Did you feel/prefer: **Or more like:**

Controlled		Emotional
Safe		Risk Taker
Corporate		Entrepreneur
Task-Oriented		Process-Oriented
Logical		Intuitive
Status Quo		Variety
Practical		Imaginative
Stability		Change
Analytical		Perceptive
Data/Facts		People

Details _____ Big Picture
Rule Bound _____ Experimental
Reserved _____ Open
　　　Total x's _____   _____   _____

Are your results similar this time? Would you have coped better by moving more toward the opposite side in each case? Or by using a combination?

In doing these exercises notice:

1. Your perceptions of each change. Beth, for example, perceived her change style to be Discrete, although her changes were a mix of both Discrete and Domino characteristics. What mattered in her case was how she handled each one as a task to be completed. She organized her thoughts and planned her actions one at a time.

How do you feel you handled your changes? Did you fall apart? Feel steep ups and downs? Need a lot of support? Sense your self-esteem was threatened? Feel out of control? These feelings would weight the experience more toward the Domino end of the Continuum.

2. There are no right or wrong answers. The purpose is to show where your major changes fall on the Continuum and give you added insight into your responses and coping mechanisms. This forms the basis for learning about your coping style.

Progress Report

In the Preface I promised you new research and theory. If you're like Allison, you like to have the facts on a topic. She preferred looking at her life analytically, trying to figure out what caused her changes. She liked massaging the information, weighing it and prioritizing it.

Beth liked the practical aspects. A doer, she liked using categories and lists to put things in sequence and set goals for her future.

Carole liked learning things and applying them in practical ways. After trying the exercises on herself, she discussed them with friends.

Diana loved the stories of other women's lives. She empathized with other women, and imagined using "the Domino theory," as she called it, in a story.

Elinor was taken with the trends and the complexity of change. She related this information to her future, both for her personal life and her business, where trend spotting is essential. She also loved the Change Continuum because it helped her understand her Domino events and how she brought chaos on herself sometimes.

Doing the exercises makes planning for your future easier too. As you understand more about who you are you can build upon your past experiences.

Next you'll identify your coping style and see how it affects your life choices, ambitions and relationships.

CHAPTER II

Five Coping Styles

OVERVIEW

Have you been described as "highly logical"? Or perhaps "very well organized"?

Long before I undertook my research on responses to change, I noticed distinct differences in the way people cope with things that happen. Some individuals consistently analyze while others express how they feel about things. Others organize readily and still others leap to action. There are also those who are hard to categorize because they match their style to different situations.

You've probably made similar observations. Personality types are anything but new. In addition to Myers-Briggs, I've relied on learning theorists Patricia Cross, David Kolb and Bernice McCarthy. The ideas of John Holland, Ned Herrmann and Dudley Lynch, among others, have contributed to my thinking too.

In my research, I found individuals describe their life changes and coping strategies in different ways. Each person was likely to repeat actions that had worked before, and similar patterns of coping soon emerged. These patterns further clarified the different responses on the Change Continuum and led to the breakdowns I'll introduce here.

As I mentioned earlier, such categories or styles are useful in research for detecting new patterns and gaining new insights. For some time, I've found these useful in helping my clients enhance their effectiveness. **Identifying your style of coping can help you see the strengths you already have and the areas in which improvement will give you more personal power.** You'll also discover specific ways you can be more effective in every aspect of your life.

Here are the coping styles I use with the names of the women who are examples of each. Allison, always analyzing, is a Logical. Well-organized Beth is a Lister. Carole, able to use all the styles and to adapt easily, is a Learner; emotional, people-oriented Diana is a Listener, and Elinor, who leaps to action, is a Leaper. Notice their positions on the Change Continuum between Discrete and Domino.

THE CHANGE CONTINUUM:
COPING STYLES

DISCRETE |——————————|——————————| DOMINO

Logical	Lister	Learner	Listener	Leaper
Allison	Beth	Carole	Diana	Elinor

EXERCISE I

IDENTIFYING YOUR COPING STYLE

First select the example for *each* situation that best describes you. Score it 3. Select a second choice that is next most like you. Score it 2. Select a third next like you. Score it 1. If you have no second or third choice, skip ahead to the next question. Don't force yourself to choose beyond the first choice if the words don't describe you.

1. I would credit my career success to my:
   A. _____ Analytical abilities.
   B. _____ Organizing and planning skills.
   C. _____ Seeking opportunities to grow.
   D. _____ People skills.
   E. _____ Creativity and ideas.
2. The way I prefer to make decisions is:
   A. _____ Weigh my options and narrow my alternatives.
   B. _____ Play it safe and go with what's worked before.

C. _____ Use a variety of strategies, whatever works.
D. _____ Trust my gut.
E. _____ Go with my intuition.

3. My résumé shows:
   A. _____ Specific career field; jobs at a few firms.
   B. _____ Me building on my strengths from year to year.
   C. _____ Moves from function to function.
   D. _____ Roles with lots of people contact.
   E. _____ Lots of moves within a creative field.

4. A large part of my work involves:
   A. _____ Working with numbers or technical data.
   B. _____ Scheduling and coordinating routine projects.
   C. _____ A mix of new projects and some routine tasks.
   D. _____ Communicating with others.
   E. _____ Coming up with new ways to do things.

5. Don't ask me, I prefer not to:
   A. _____ Counsel someone with personal problems.
   B. _____ Go out on a limb for an idea.
   C. _____ Do routine, nitty-gritty work all the time.
   D. _____ Crunch numbers and analyze the results.
   E. _____ Do the same thing from hour to hour.

6. One of my favorite activities is:
   A. _____ Solving mysteries or puzzles.
   B. _____ Organizing my possessions.
   C. _____ Learning a new way to do something.
   D. _____ Listening to a friend's story.
   E. _____ Experimenting with the latest fashions.

7. You could say that my desk:
   A. _____ Has piles, but I know where everything is.
   B. _____ Is very organized and neat.
   C. _____ Changes as my projects do.
   D. _____ Has lots of personal mementos on it.
   E. _____ Is a sea of this and that, lots of stuff.

8. My support system consists of:
   A. _____ My family and one or two friends.
   B. _____ Trained professionals and one or two friends.
   C. _____ A mix, depending on my needs.
   D. _____ A network of very warm friends.
   E. _____ An eclectic mix from my various lives.

9. When I have a problem, I:
    A. _____ Do research to get all my facts.
    B. _____ Make lists of what I must do.
    C. _____ Do a variety of things depending on the problem.
    D. _____ Talk to someone who's been through it before.
    E. _____ Brainstorm with myself to get ideas.
10. To help keep up in my field I prefer to:
    A. _____ Read technical journals.
    B. _____ Go to conferences or workshops.
    C. _____ Do whatever it takes to learn the latest.
    D. _____ Talk to others about what's happening.
    E. _____ See what my competitors are doing.

Now go back and add up the points you gave all the A's, then the B's, C's, D's and E's, recording your scores below:

Total Scores	Style
A _____	Logical
B _____	Lister
C _____	Learner
D _____	Listener
E _____	Leaper

Your top score is your preferred coping style. Do you have a close second? That's your backup style. Are three or more scores fairly equal? Then you're very versatile and switch from style to style as needed. Your lowest scores may indicate styles you're avoiding. Make a special note of those. You'll learn more about each style as we go along.

THE FIVE STYLES

The five women are models for the coping styles. You'll find out more about each one and you'll learn how each applied her particular coping skills to her crisis: Allison with her work-family conflict, Beth with her divorce and job loss, Carole with her burnout, Diana with her cancer scare and Elinor with getting fired. You'll see too how their styles affect nearly everything in their lives.

Logical

If you're a Logical, you want all the facts. You're analytical, good with numbers and consider endless options when coping with a problem. You never fail to ask "what if," considering the various consequences of a choice. You think long and hard before making major changes in your life, and tend to be loyal to your profession and to your employer. You might be in law, financial analysis, engineering, systems analysis, computer programming or another area where your reserve, precision and critical thinking are valued. You bring an analytical focus to everything, even a personal crisis or dilemma.

Allison, the energy company lawyer, was a Logical. She always needed to know the reasons why something was so, and she enjoyed tasks that challenged her logical and analytical abilities. She showed these abilities as a child and developed them through the study of math, science and, eventually, law.

"In the beginning, I liked the adversarial nature of law; I enjoyed wrestling to define issues," she said. Combining her science background and her legal training "made sense," as she put it.

She and her husband Keith, an engineer, were among the first to have a computer at home. "It's so much faster," she told me. "Now I key in the variables, assign different weights and sort through a lot of data very fast."

Picture her some years earlier as a young mother, tired but glowing, as she lifted the blue blanket and looked adoringly at the newborn in her arms. She told herself that her mind didn't have to go soft just because she had a new baby boy, reminding herself that she had worked very hard to become a lawyer and to have a respected position with a major energy company. She'd only been there a year when she became pregnant with her second child.

"I didn't dare let them know I was pregnant at first. I hadn't cared at the law firm, but now I was at a company where I hoped to stay and advance. I'm tall, but eventually people notice. After a while, I could no longer hide it!" She smiled at the memory. "The women at the office were suddenly wonderful to me. They'd been a little aloof before and I didn't go out of my way to get involved in the gossip or the birthday lunches. But suddenly, I became one of them! No longer 'one of the boys.' "

True to her Logical style, she deliberated the possible consequence of each action: staying home longer, working a part-time schedule, asking for a transfer. "What if? . . . But on the other hand . . ." She didn't need to write things down as her razor-sharp mind sorted through the options.

Much as she liked efficiency, Allison would never rush to a conclusion, as would Elinor, a Leaper. Faced with her conflicts over leaving her new baby to return to work, she gathered facts about live-in help and various types of day care. She read what the experts said, compared costs and weighed what she thought her boss's reaction would be to each choice.

During our interview at her comfortable suburban home in Teaneck, New Jersey, Allison wore jeans and an oversized sweatshirt and no makeup. She showed me around the house and mentioned that they hoped to build an addition to it. Then we retired to her study, which had ships in bottles, wood paneling, lots of books and a pair of armchairs in front of the fireplace. She noted that the ships in bottles had been her father's. She served me hot apple cider and Toll-House cookies as we concentrated on her story.

With her daughter Kathy, she had planned to stay home for six months. They were fortunate in finding a warm, reliable woman who took care of Kathy so that Allison could go to law school, she explained. "With Scotty it was different. We needed the money, and I had to make it clear at my company that I wanted to be taken seriously."

She presented a proposal to spend three days a week in her office, taking home contracts to review. After two months, she'd return to work full-time. Negotiating with her boss, she stressed advantages to the company and her commitment to a long-term career. It worked.

I asked her, "If you had to make that decision today, how would you do it differently?"

"Oh, I'd have even more options today. Women are striking deals of all kinds!" She went on to describe some of the deals in her precise Logical manner.

In a crisis, Allison would normally identify the problem, then go about solving it in a rational way. Her feelings about leaving her baby were beyond the realm of reason, which made this crisis difficult for her.

For a Logical, the pain in a crisis comes from things not making sense. More recently, witnessing her father's rapid deterioration from Alzheimer's disease, Allison found her coping skills challenged. They were challenged too when her adorable baby boy grew up to be a defiant teenager who used illegal drugs. As we'll see later, Logical skills alone didn't provide the answers Allison needed.

Like every other style, Logicals have their strengths and problems too.

YOUR LOGICAL STRENGTHS AND PROBLEMS

Which of these is true for you? Check *only* the ones that seem to fit.

True for You

1. I can get bogged down in details.   _____
2. While others may give up on a problem, I tend to stick it out and persevere to a rational solution.   _____
3. Sometimes I concentrate on the trees while missing the forest.   _____
4. I'm good at anticipating problems and generating alternative ways to reach a goal.   _____
5. I relish abstractions and can forget the consequences for myself and others.   _____
6. I cut through emotional issues and get to the facts underlying why something is wrong.   _____
7. Others may ask questions to be making conversation. I ask a question to get an answer.   _____
8. People say I treat them fairly and weigh all sides of a situation before making a recommendation.   _____

Total   _____

If you checked five or more, your style includes some Logical behaviors.

Lister

Yes, you're a list-maker. Outlining or organizing things yields a sense of control so necessary to your well-being. You're good at details, you ferret out the things other people miss. You're realistic, reliable and practical. You're not known for your creativity because you're preoccupied with playing it safe. As a manager or administrator, you're highly effective, however, because you focus on getting things done. Employers value the skills you bring to the workplace. These traits also make you a valuable partner or friend.

Beth, the professor turned training specialist, was a Lister. Her office and her apartment were meticulously organized. Even in the worst crisis, she busied herself itemizing, indexing, cataloging, sorting things out. Sometimes, living with her alcoholic husband, she straightened her cupboards top to bottom while trying to sort out her thoughts and feelings.

Knowing that he was not about to stop drinking and that she must leave him, Beth finally said to herself, "I *will* get through this. I *will* survive. I've just got to stay calm and take it one step at a time." Then, she sat at her desk to make a "to do" list. Give notice at the college . . . find a temporary place to stay . . . make plans for move. "I remember so well, as I was trying to decide what to take with me, I realized I knew which were his favorite books and records, so I listed the ones I especially wanted."

Once she figured out what she was going to do next and what followed that, she started to feel better.

"I'm really organized," she said, showing off a tiny closet in her apartment. The closet held winter coats, hatboxes, gift wrap, a wide assortment of things arranged in boxes, bins, on hooks and hangers, even strung from the ceiling. Everything was visible, and with her folding step stool, accessible. It was a marvel of arrangement that I couldn't help but admire.

Her minimally furnished apartment was elegant. Her antiques, the wood gleaming with polish, were arranged in groupings on beige Oriental carpets. Showing me to one of two wingback chairs in a corner, she served iced tea with fresh mint in tall crystal glasses. The coasters for guests to use were handy. No detail was overlooked. She obviously preferred classic clothing and traditional furniture to avant-garde or trendy things. "I'm quite thrifty too. I have sweaters I bought in the seventies. Maybe because I was a depression baby and my parents didn't have much. My mother worked hard for me to go to a good college, and to help me in graduate school too," she noted.

Even on a Saturday, her curly, graying brown hair was freshly coiffed, her tweeds and cotton shirt pressed, her loafers polished. "I think my neatness stems from our family situation. You see, my father drank. Our home was very chaotic. I was always afraid of setting him off or upsetting the delicate balance in some way. I'm happiest when things are tranquil and pleasant and predictable.

"Then I married a man who turned out to be an alcoholic too, when the going got rough and the university didn't give him tenure. I could see how weak he was. Why else does a man strike a woman, the woman he loves? Weakness, powerlessness . . . Anyway, his behavior made me angry and I found strength in that anger. I resolved to go straight ahead one step at a time with my plans."

She read a book on divorce, hired a tough lawyer, moved in with friends to finish out the semester and made plans for the move to New York. "There was so much to do. Every day I made a list and crossed things off. I don't know how people function without lists, especially when a lot is happening all at once."

I posed the question, "Knowing what you know now, would you do anything differently?"

"I'd be a lot kinder to myself," she said softly. "Not try so hard for control. I'd beat a pillow or let out a scream now and then." Her eyes twinkled. "On second thought, I wouldn't scream. The neighbors would think I was being attacked!" She slapped the arm of her chair, suppressing her rebel yell.

When I noted her designation as a Lister, she nodded in recognition. "I've got lists on my lists," she laughed. "On my refrigerator, in my date book and in my purse. In October I start my calendar for the next year. I keep files at home on topics that interest me—exhibits to see, books to look into, places I want to visit, courses I want to take. I even have articles on basic home repair!"

In a crisis, a Lister feels real pain when things become chaotic and out of control. If you're like Beth, you can face even the most difficult situation by sitting down and mapping out what steps to take. Even in a life and death situation, you draw up a list. Let's see if your strengths and problems are those of a Lister.

EXERCISE III

YOUR LISTER STRENGTHS AND PROBLEMS

True for You

1. My time-management skills help me accomplish a lot in less time than others.   _____
2. I get upset when things get mislaid or lost or forgotten.   _____
3. People rely on me to be calm in a crisis.   _____
4. I can bring order to chaotic situations.   _____
5. I spend time keeping my records in order and labeled too.   _____
6. I'm nervous about being late for appointments and sometimes arrive too early.   _____

7. I always put things in writing "for the files."   _____
8. I like to be in control of situations.   _____

Total   _____

A score of five or more means there's a Lister in you too!

Listers, like Logicals, look at life changes as one-at-a-time events, problems that are manageable. Yet some Listers and Logicals have difficulty understanding other people's feelings and why there are conflicts. Their lists may not include subtler, emotional considerations that are important too.

Corporations in the seventies sought Logical and Lister behaviors. As we might expect, more men have Lister and Logical coping styles. From an early age, they're trained not to show emotions and they're socialized to be logical and orderly in their thinking. Perhaps you've noticed these differences in colleagues, bosses, relatives and lovers.

Listener

You may call yourself a communicator and may work as one, like Diana. In touch with your own emotions, you easily empathize with the feelings of others. You make friends and build professional alliances easily. In a team situation, you tune in to what makes everyone work well together. You can inspire, motivate and influence people too. You genuinely like people, and you want people to like you.

You may also be good at public speaking, and be able to express yourself orally or in writing in ways that people quickly grasp. You are effective in traditionally female "helping" professions such as teaching, nursing and social work, but increasingly women Listeners do well in medicine, psychotherapy, corporate training, selling, motivating and negotiating.

As a Listener, Diana's first reaction to a health crisis was emotional: "Oh my God, I'll never live to see Jason grow up! Nate will have to raise him alone. My novel will never be written!" Then a little later, when thinking about taking sick leave from her job: "What can I tell them at work? My boss wants me to write that important speech and I'll be in the hospital by the time he needs the final draft. I don't dare let him down. What if it leaks out that this is cancer surgery? They might find some excuse to replace me with someone younger, healthier!"

"Those were the things I thought to myself. 'I have to get used to this,' I told myself, then I thought, 'No, I don't *want* to get used to this!' "

When I visited at her Park Slope Victorian home, it was several years after her scare. "Yes, I cried and I raged. I thought I was dying. . . . I wondered if I'd have six weeks or six years."

She offered me cream soda and nachos on lacquered trays. Her cocktail table was buried under a heap of magazines. Children's toys were parked nearby and a few dust bunnies huddled in a corner.

"I cried for days. This is the kid who used to risk her life rock climbing! Death never seemed real to me until that day in the doctor's office.

"I don't know what I'd have done without my family and friends to see me through my surgery. I couldn't talk to people at work about my problem. That was hard on me. But other women who'd had hysterectomies seemed to come out of the woodwork. I realized I wasn't alone."

Diana nestled deeper into the brightly colored pillows on her sofa. "I'll never know if people at the office bought my appendectomy story. But they were very sweet. They sent flowers and kept me up to date on everything, even the gossip."

"What do you feel you'd do differently, knowing what you know now?" I asked.

"I'd get the facts. Not panic, the way I did. Not let my emotions get the better of me. The cells were precancerous, not cancerous. It was a very threatening situation, but I wasn't at death's door as I'd thought. Nate talked to the doctor himself, then insisted on getting a second opinion. Both doctors recommended surgery as a precaution. It was a partial hysterectomy. They left my ovaries."

Three-year-old Kimmy climbed on her lap for a kiss. "Here's my healer," Diana sighed, then the child made a beeline for the playroom where her brother Jason was playing a video game.

Diana and Nate adopted Kimmy after Diana had fully recovered from the surgery.

She talked easily, showing no embarrassment, only vestiges of her intense, emotional pain. She'd used her story to help others having a rough time; telling it was an important part of her psychic recovery. Notice that Diana didn't think of looking for answers to her medical problem at the library or on a data base. Instead, she called her friends. Just like a woman, some might say. But certainly not all women.

Diana's Listener skills enabled her to relate well to others in her jobs and in her personal life as well. "My Jewish in-laws had grave doubts about me. Nate had been burned by his first marriage so he was a bit wary too. But we had such good times together, so many laughs, that we wanted to go on, have kids, do the whole bit." She blushed as she looked out at her pudgy, balding husband now working diligently in the yard.

During their engagement, Diana, who'd been baptized Catholic but had essentially no religion, studied Judaism with a rabbi. She not only learned to cook a traditional Jewish meal, she went to every Bar and Bas Mitzvah. She learned all she could about each member of Nate's family and did small favors for them whenever she could: a clipping about stamp collecting for Nate's father, some special-order silver pieces for his mother and carefully chosen samples of her company's cosmetics for all the family. By the time Jason was born, they'd warmed to her, and when she had her hysterectomy two years later, they were at her bedside with long-stemmed roses.

People were happy to have Diana around. When something went wrong, she sensed it and helped smooth things over. When in trouble, she would reach out to friends, seeking the help and support she'd given them.

If you're a Listener like Diana, you like to tell and to hear stories in almost any circumstances. You'd rather meet face to face with people than write memos. You mirror their body language subtly and reflect their feelings as you speak. Your greatest pain in a crisis is confronting negativity and loss, especially loss of relationships. At one time, Diana was deeply hurt if someone gave her negative criticism. Eventually she learned to put things in perspective although she still feared losing loved ones and friends. She was distressed too when relationships with colleagues ended and when conflicts couldn't be bridged. Losing her uterus and, with it, the chance of bearing more children, was very difficult for her emotionally, even after she learned she would not lose her life.

EXERCISE IV

YOUR LISTENER STRENGTHS AND PROBLEMS

True for You

1. I become so involved with people that I don't always make the best business decisions.   _____

2. People count on me to empathize and listen to their
   problems.   _____
3. Maintaining relationships is more important to me
   than other issues at stake.   _____
4. I can sense from people's body language how they're
   reacting in a meeting.   _____
5. I'm not as well organized as others and often get
   behind on paperwork.   _____
6. Friends ask me for advice in resolving interpersonal
   conflicts.   _____
7. Persuading others is one of my skills.   _____
8. I get upset when others are unhappy over something
   I've done.   _____

                                              Total   _____

If you've checked five or more, there's some Listener in your style.

We all need Listeners in our lives. The traditional wife was a good
Listener. Some contemporary women, for better or for worse, have suppressed this aspect of themselves. Men today are becoming better Listeners, often at the insistence of the women in their lives.

Leaper

If you're a Leaper, you jump in where others fear to tread, often without
looking. You're intuitive and conceptual, good at improvising. You can
pull diverse elements together into a synthesis, and have an eye for the big
picture. You create images as you think. You may move fast, even impul-
sively, as Elinor did.

She puffed up a storm, pacing her tiny apartment in a frenzy about
what to do next. "So I was fired. It happens to everyone, right? Then why
do I feel so desperate? I've always gotten jobs before. I could always use
my parents' contacts and work in a pharmacy, but that's a last resort. I'm
further along now. Things are tougher too."

She picked up her phone in one hand, her Rolodex in the other and
started flipping the cards. The first number she reached belonged to
someone who was out of the country. She'd forgotten. Flipping to another
card, she dialed again. On some days, she opened the Rolodex at random,
in hopes of inspiration. One such inspiration found her a place to sleep in
New York. Though impulsive, she was also original, innovative, indepen-

dent and competitive. Fond of color, she used drawings to code things and "mind map" her plans.

If you're like Elinor, you might work in advertising, marketing, new product development or strategic planning. You might also be an entrepreneur, a small business operator or free-lancer. Elinor learned the retailing business working in the pharmacy her parents owned before they retired, but now, only a few years later, she found returning to such an atmosphere unthinkable. Her friends now were artists and she moved comfortably in the world of avant-garde fashion.

She welcomed me into her small one-room apartment. Barefoot in an emerald sari, she reclined on her muslin futon as though posing for a fashion shot. Her eclectic array of belongings crowded the tiny space. Hats from around the world covered one wall, intricate teak carvings adorned another. Swatches of fabric, photos, posters and prints were all interestingly yet tightly arranged, leaving no space unused. A parachute hung harem-style above our heads. She didn't show me her closet. I imagined that it contained as much as Beth's but that things might tumble out when the door was opened.

The air was filled with incense. I could only guess at what the sandlewood scent was supposed to mask.

Elinor would typically break the rules for the fun of it, and she took other chances too. "Sometimes I take too many risks." She inhaled on her brown cigarette. "With men . . . with my life. God, I hope I don't get AIDS. I haven't taken that many chances, but if I don't live to be old, I'd really like to feel that I'd enjoyed all there was to enjoy, know what I mean?"

She offered me jug wine and a plate of crackers that turned out to be stale.

"I take risks in my work too. I have to try things that are different. I love adventure. I sure didn't think New Haven was a big risk. . . . I mean, I might have gone to Calcutta or Beirut. But New Haven?" She made a face.

In a crisis the Leaper feels pain (and even panic) at lack of clarity. If you're a Leaper, you usually want a lucid picture of how things are or how they will be. Although your vision of the world has room for some ambiguity and chaos, you feel anxious and frustrated when things become fuzzy and confusing. When Elinor lost her job, it was far from clear how she would earn a living or where or how she would live. Yet one feels she dreaded working in a pharmacy more than, say, camping out in Central Park.

One of the few things you fear if you're a Leaper is boredom, but your striving for excitement may blind you to some common-sense choices. You may also be such an idea generator that you confuse others who'd prefer sound reasoning over creativity. Your pace and your style of communicating can leave other people's heads spinning. You'd do well to try to see their points of view.

I asked Elinor about the job search. "I was spinning my wheels at first. Bouncing off the walls in all directions. I didn't plan. I could always work in a pharmacy again—death by prescription! That reminds me, somebody was supposed to call me about a manufacturer's rep job—I'd forgotten all about it. I'd better start keeping track of things." Leapers often function best alongside a Lister assistant to organize things for them.

"So what would you do differently next time around?" I asked.

"Please, I don't want to do this again. I'm too old."

I couldn't help thinking—*at twenty-eight?* I saw her take the last of the crackers.

"Next time I'd have Plan B, you know, in case Plan A doesn't work. I'd have some money stashed away." She changed the subject. "How about a nosh?" Then she stared at the empty refrigerator shelves.

That's my Elinor, I thought. Is she you?

EXERCISE V

YOUR LEAPER STRENGTHS AND PROBLEMS

	True for You
1. My impulsiveness has made my career "checkered."	_____
2. I'm great at improvising at the last minute.	_____
3. I find Logicals and Listers boring.	_____
4. My enthusiasm is infectious.	_____
5. I don't take time to give my subordinates step-by-step directions.	_____
6. I'm more creative than many people I know.	_____
7. I see more possibilities and relationships between different elements than others do.	_____

8. I sometimes see so many options that I can't decide
   which is best.   _____

                                        Total   _____

   A score of five or more means there's a Leaper in your actions.

Fortunately, large organizations are finally appreciating Leapers, although many have left for smaller firms or their own businesses. Intrapreneurism (entrepreneurial behavior within a large corporation) and participative management call for Leapers and Listeners too. Many companies were launched by Leapers who brought in Logicals and Listers to structure a business and manage it.

Effective organizations need people with all these coping styles. Each task force, project team or group needs all four.

Problems arise when we stick to just one style. When we insist upon thinking only logically, narrowly, emotionally or intuitively, we miss what others are saying and we fail to get our point across to people who think differently.

We also get in trouble because we don't understand why others aren't more like us. When we're aware of someone else's style and how it clashes with ours, we can change our behavior to shorten the distance between us. We can build a bridge that makes for better communication. Carole, as a Learner, knew how to match others' styles.

Carole Shares a Secret from Sales

Sales and marketing people learn to identify these or similar personality types so they can win acceptance and communicate with different people. If you work in one of these fields you may have already dealt with customers as types. If this is new to you, you may be amazed at how much sharp salespeople and marketing executives seem to know about you.

Our friend Carole was a marketer and a good one at that. We've seen her in the middle of a Domino crisis, suffering from job burnout shortly after the breakup with her boyfriend and the death of her mother. We'll be seeing much more of her too. First let's watch her flexibility and her marketing skills in action as we see how she would sell something to the other four.

Selling Logical Allison a product like a smart card, Carole would do a comparative analysis: "This card is better than 'a' because it does this,

this and this, which no other card does." Allison might also comparison shop, but she would decide on something quickly if she needed it and it made sense to her.

To appeal to the Lister like Beth, Carole would provide the facts: "This card costs you 'x' amount at an annual rate of 'z.' With this card you are admitted rapidly at hospitals. It has your medical records on it. Wherever you are in the world, you can get credit because it has your credit history on it." The fine print in the ads interests the Lister. Listers don't make up their minds quickly; they're most likely to want more details and to shop around.

To hook a Listener like Diana, Carole might play on her emotions. "This card will provide for your family in an emergency, protect them from theft and cover them with additional life and accident insurance. You'll feel better once you have it." Face to face, she'd gain Diana's confidence with an exchange of small talk, then patiently answer Diana's questions.

She would approach a Leaper like Elinor by painting pictures of what a smart card could do for her. She would use phrases like "Imagine having the latest accessory before anyone else, the glamour this card can give you." Her ads would show illustrations of savvy, sophisticated trendsetters using the card. Elinor would probably succumb whether she needed it or not.

The next time someone zeros in on you and seems to know just where you're coming from, how you think and what your values are, stop and admire her skills. Direct-sales people do this face to face with prospects. Marketers like Carole do it in print and media; interviewers do it to get a sense of your "fit" in an organization.

You too can move into styles very different from your own, using them in any situation—job interviews, when asking your boss for a raise, when confronting your spouse or your lover.

Learner

As a Learner, Carole could glide easily from one type to another. Having learned to communicate with all types of people, she had an edge in virtually any situation. People didn't usually know *why* she was effective; they just knew that she was. In a social situation, though, others noticed how she drew out different types of people.

How did Carole become so versatile in coping? I asked her to talk about her background.

"I've always enjoyed learning. I think 'learn' was my mother's favorite word, my father's too. We took advantage of the cultural opportunities available in Chicago. We always had books from the library, went to the Field Museum and the Art Institute, and I took special classes in both science and art. But that's not all."

She showed me pictures from her childhood of Carole and her two sisters in exotic costumes. "My mother would have us play 'United Nations.' I think she tried out her classroom activities on us."

We were settled on the modern convertible sofa in her airy, plant-filled third-floor walkup. Her soft print robe blended with the creams and corals of the upholstery. Ebony African masks watched us from one wall.

"My father encouraged me to develop some business sense. My sisters and I sold home products door to door besides baby-sitting and the things kids usually do to earn money—I should say things kids *used* to do!" She laughed, then continued, "He taught me to count up what I earned, spend a portion of it and save something too. My sisters preferred to play with their dolls. Maybe I was Daddy's 'son' since there weren't any boys in our family, but there was never any doubt that I was a girl." She showed me a photo of her father at the Merchandise Mart in his security uniform.

"Then I guess I developed 'street smarts.' You have to, growing up black in a big city. You have to have 'street smarts' if you're black or a woman and especially if you're both. You have to be savvy about how you behave, how to fit in *if* you want to make it in a world different from your own."

She poured more sangria and passed a plate of fresh vegetables with a mild curry and yogurt dip. We crunched in unison.

"Leaving the neighborhood to work in the Loop at a major bank was a big step for me. I put on a navy blue suit, and I look terrible in navy blue, but it helped me fit in. I watched my speech. Fortunately, my parents spoke middle-class-educated English but my friends didn't always. It wasn't easy, but I knew from my parents there was such a thing as 'getting ahead' and that's what I wanted.

"Having an M.B.A. helps too, but the reality of being a token and a minority taught me down-in-the-trenches survival tactics that are beyond books. Every time I had a setback, I'd find out where I went wrong. And I learned to hide my emotions, box them up for later!"

Her education—in and out of school—and her experience in the financial world helped her develop Logical and Lister abilities. She wasn't as cold or dry as these types can sometimes be, however. She was empathic and aware of others as Listeners are. She had the conceptual and creative aspects of a Leaper that enabled her to dream up new marketing campaigns, but she wasn't as scattered as some Leapers seem to be.

She told me that she had been seeing a therapist, also a black woman, as she came to terms with the breakup with Malcolm, her boyfriend, and the death of her mother. "I've got to get it together," she'd told herself. After kicking Malcolm out, she'd lectured herself, echoing what her sister told her on the phone, "Do it for Mama." Then, shaking her head, summoning her self-reliance, she vowed to herself, "For Mama and for me too. I'm gonna be a lot stronger and a lot smarter when this is over."

That's the attitude of a Learner.

Because of a recurring back problem Carole went to a support group of people with bad backs. She also found time to be active in professional groups and took an interest in several causes.

She was a good Listener wherever she happened to be. She didn't lean too heavily on other people's ideas, though, because she knew to trust her own.

She didn't panic, not at the breakup of her relationship or at her mother's passing away. She coped with her Domino upheaval using all four styles. Since she was closer to the Listener/Leaper end of the Continuum, these skills came more naturally to her. In a crisis she found it harder to be as calm or rational as Logical Allison would be.

The true Logical or the Lister caught in a situation like Carole's might describe it like this: "My mother died, which was very hard. That was at about the same time I broke up with the man I'd been living with. I felt a certain dissatisfaction with my job too. Of course, none of these things relate to any of the others and they all had to be dealt with separately."

Eventually, Carole too isolated her problems and dealt with each in turn. But not before she'd experienced the total Domino impact that made her ask herself. *"What's the meaning of all this? What must I learn before going on with my life?"*

Learn What You've Avoided

Your company may take your style into account, even providing feedback from superiors, co-workers and subordinates about gaps in your abilities. Perhaps you've been given a hint of strengths or deficiencies in a performance review. You might even be slotted into an area where you could get the experience to fill in the gaps. But don't wait for that to happen. **Take**

responsibility for your own career and develop the styles you've avoided in the past so you can plot your *own* career course.

Most people are more complex than the types I've presented here. You probably already function outside of your primary style, using the skills of two or even three. That's good, far better than being stuck in one. Yet if you're like a lot of people, one of the styles is difficult. It's just "not you." It's your blind spot, so you end up avoiding tasks and behaviors related to that style. Doing so can hold you back in your career or undermine your relationships.

For example, Diana would put off filing papers and balancing her checkbook. You might shy away from people of a certain style too. Elinor avoided the company of men and women who fit into the Logical category.

By avoiding one style, you're diminishing your potential. Like an engine running on three cylinders instead of four, you're only using seventy-five percent of the power you might be using. Using them all can get you closer to the hundred percent solution, and can get you much more of what you want in your career and relationships.

Now look again at Exercise I at the beginning of this chapter. As I noted, your scores also reveal your most avoided style or styles. Discovering what you avoid is extremely valuable in understanding yourself and the things that can go wrong in your life.

But you can change. You can learn your way out of this situation. Here are ways to acquire competencies in the areas where you're less adept and less comfortable. I'm suggesting that you learn competencies as opposed to skills. Skills are what you can do, while competencies are what you can *demonstrate* through your achievements.

Logical Competencies

If you suspect you've avoided Logical skills, begin by studying the technical aspects of your field. Elinor had to learn open-to-buy and other mathematical aspects of retailing. If you're one of the many victims of math anxiety, buy a computer teaching program and play games requiring math skill. Start being meticulous about your checkbook; calculate the percentage of markdowns as you shop for bargains. Learning by yourself is fun for some, but if it isn't for you, hire a tutor. Listeners especially enjoy learning with a tutor or in a class. To acquire an avoided competency, Leapers need to see how it fits into the big picture of their lives. They also need to make learning a creative challenge.

Lister Competencies

Diana, strikingly lacking in Lister skills, needed better organization and discipline to succeed as a free-lancer someday. Also, she knew that she didn't understand the family finances well enough to get along if something happened to her husband, Nate. Her first step was to buy an organizer-calendar and a set of colored pens for writing down different things she had to do. She started a filing system at home, coding items with different colored files.

She also accompanied Nate to the office of the accountant who worked for his business. Because she liked him, she took a greater interest in tax write-offs and profit-sharing plans. She also considered taking a course in finance because she learned well in a group situation.

If you resemble Diana, you can tackle things you've avoided if you can make them fun. Sometimes a new calendar or colored pens will do the trick. As a Listener, you may find you can perform the toughest tasks with other people around to support you. You'll enjoy support groups and classes. Hiring an expert to help you organize your time or your possessions can make a real impact on your life too.

Listener Competencies

Allison, on the other hand, needed to develop empathy and sensitivity to others. Her children taught her to be more responsive, she said. She made her greatest strides, however, in support groups that forced her to face her own emotional responses to personal problems.

If you resemble Allison, you can develop your "people" skills in a number of different ways. Besides support groups, try joining professional organizations, networks, business organizations, activist groups and political groups where you can interact with others. Coaching and mentoring others is also valuable. Personal growth seminars help push aside the mask you wear and show you how your behavior affects others.

Leaper Competencies

Perhaps you're a Lister or a Logical in need of more creativity. In my department-store days, I once had an assistant buyer who lacked a sense of style—a real liability in women's wear. I asked her to shop different stores and report on the colors, styles and labels. Then we shopped the market together. Soon she assembled better displays that made shoppers stop and take notice. Not only that, she found her own "look" and replaced her frumpy clothes with flattering ones. She had the abilities; they just needed to be developed.

Beth enhanced her creativity by enrolling in an art class in mixed media. She found it fun to be less in control. Others have stirred their hidden talents by using books, tapes or seminars to learn guided imagery, brainstorming or mind mapping.

Achievers especially avoid things they aren't good at. It's not easy for a highly respected Logical executive to be floundering in an art class, paint on her face, her canvas looking like mud or worse. Or for a creative, independent person to be lost in a sea of numbers trying to master business math. But if you get through those embarrassing or difficult moments, you can achieve a great deal more. Once you make progress in an area where you've always been weak, you start to feel very, very good about yourself.

This is a good time to jot down your ideas for improvement. Rounding out your coping repertoire will open up many more options and perhaps restore some of what you've been missing or suppressing in what you're doing.

EXERCISE VI

YOUR DEVELOPMENTAL PLAN

I plan to develop the _____ style(s) by

_____

Now let's look at another situation where flexibility in your style can pay a dividend:

EXERCISE VII

ACING YOUR INTERVIEW

Practice your flexibility by imagining yourself interviewing for a job with each of the five women. Be aware of each woman's style.

How would you impress each one? What would you wear, knowing her field and company? How would you demonstrate your competencies to advantage? Think about this a moment. Jot down your ideas before reading my suggestions on what to do.

Their Style	Your Strategy
Logical Allison	_____
Lister Beth	_____
Learner Carole	_____
Listener Diana	_____
Leaper Elinor	_____

SUGGESTIONS FOR YOUR INTERVIEW

First, you're face to face with *Logical Allison*. Conservative dress is best here, but she won't pay much attention to what you're wearing. She might be formal or reserved and fail to put you at ease. She might toss you a problem to solve right off the bat. Show her that you know your field and that your mind is sharp. She'll soon know if you have what it takes. She might ask for some facts about your education and experience but will cut you off as soon as she's heard enough. She might show some wit or she might be quite reserved; follow her example. The odd thing is you probably won't have a clue as to whether the interview went well or not!

Now you're up against *Lister Beth*, at another large bureaucratic organization. Right away you'd be struck by her efficient, no-nonsense quest for details. You'd tick off your accomplishments and the results of your actions to show that you're a doer. You'd be practical and to the point, without digressions. She'd want to know how you got from "a" to "b." You'd want to show her that you're reliable. Her interview might be shorter than the others. You'd wear something conservative in this situation too, and you'd better be there on time.

Next, *Listener Diana* is interviewing you for a job in a large consumer products organization. An outfit with fairly conservative lines but with a bright, becoming accent would be appropriate. She creates an easy intimacy, encourages you to divulge something personal. You feel more relaxed than with the others. If you want to impress her, you'll swap success stories with her or tell her how you overcame a people problem. The Listener will have a gut feeling about you from the beginning and your behavior will confirm it or not. Of all the styles, she's more tolerant of those unlike her, recognizing that it takes different styles to build a team.

If *Leaper Elinor* is interviewing you for a creative job in her department, you'd demonstrate your flair and originality in what you wear. She's looking for ideas and surprises. You'd illustrate with examples of your solutions to problems with images, catching her imagination. To show you're on her wavelength, you'd rev up your enthusiasm and verbal pace to match hers.

Chances are, you've already had experiences like some of these. If you're Elinor and you've just made a presentation to Allison, you might walk away thinking she was a very cold fish who wouldn't be any fun to work with. Allison, on the other hand, might see Elinor as a total flake who couldn't be counted on.

Generally, the further away you are from someone on the Continuum, the more you'll have to stretch to communicate with and impress that person. Allison and Beth would relate to each other quite well. So would Elinor and Diana. Diana was more adept than the other three at communicating and understanding, although Carole exceeded them all.

When presenting yourself to a group of people, you need to touch all four bases as *Learner Carole* did when marketing her bank to the public. Carole would gather facts about her bank's customers like a good Lister and analyze trends with her Logical abilities. She'd visualize and conceptualize new possibilities in true Leaper fashion. She'd listen to her staff and her customers, communicating in a warm Listener style. She'd ask a variety of questions, would look for all these competencies in an interview and would be aware of what you're avoiding. She'd want to be sure you could learn your way through new challenges she'd throw at you.

And in any interview you're ahead of the game if you've done your homework on the culture of each company and talked to people who've worked there.

If you're beginning to get a sense of how your style affects the achieving of your ambitions, you're getting the point. Probably your career rewards your primary style or styles. But the more flexibility you have, and the more you function as a Learner, the greater success you'll have in every aspect of your life and career.

Coping as Learning

As Carole knew so well, learning is not just school or books or even specific knowledge. It's a lifelong attitude, an ongoing awareness that makes you more skilled and more capable with each experience you have. **Certain experiences, what I've labeled "major changes," are more than simply things that happen. They're incidents that trigger times of learning. They can be turning points that shape your ambitions and your destiny. They enable you to behave in new ways. They may even provide insights that alter the way you see the past.**

Often, the more difficult the event, the more you learn. Successful people know this. Their setbacks have seasoned and strengthened them.

Allison would learn the most from those things that didn't make sense to her Logical mind: the deterioration of her once brilliant father with Alzheimer's and the drastic changes in her son as he experimented with drugs.

Beth has already learned her hardest lessons facing the lack of control she experienced when she knew that her academic career and her marriage were both at an end. She eventually became better able to tolerate uncertainty, something that is hard for a Lister to do.

Diana's toughest test was the surgery—losing her uterus—as well as fearing for her life and abandoning forever the chance of bearing more children. Trite as it may sound, she could appreciate being alive more than before. As a Listener, she was still emotional, but she didn't panic as easily anymore.

Elinor wilted at the lack of clarity in a difficult situation and feared boredom beyond all else. Distress at being out of work, out of money and out of town caused this Leaper to become more practical with backup plans and emergency money.

In real learning, we move through the pain. In a crisis, stop long enough to ask yourself these questions: What is really bothering me most? What is really important here?

You may not immediately identify what's going on. You may have to work up to making your move. Sometimes you're in a sink-or-swim situation that calls for action . . . now! However things are, whatever your crisis is like, you'll end up learning, although the lesson may not be apparent until the crisis is over.

These are the lessons of adulthood, these experiences that make us

wise, mature and seasoned people. We become better players in the game of life. The Logical plays well and plays to win, yet has setbacks nonetheless. The Lister follows the rules, playing the hand she's dealt, not taking big risks. The Listener acts on gut feeling, reads body language and facial expressions, but ultimately cares more about the other players than about winning. The Leaper breaks old rules, dreams up new ones and plays wild cards.

The Learner asks, "What can I learn from this game?" and "Where can I find a more interesting, challenging game?"

You too can have multiple options and styles for approaching *your* game. Look again at your scores in all of the exercises. If three or more of your scores are fairly equal, you're close to being a Learner already, or you're one, of course, if your highest scores are in the Learner category. At any rate, you now have the information you need to fill in gaps in your coping style and play your game with greater facility.

PROGRESS REPORT

Here are the ways the five women look at the coping styles:

"The emotions seemed silly at first," said Logical Allison. "But I see your point. I need to bite my tongue and not be so quick to judge. I learned that some things are important even if they don't add up logically. I need to give feelings higher priority."

"The Leaper was too messy for me," offered Lister Beth, "yet I envy her daring sometimes. That style exercise really pegged me although I don't much like the name 'Lister.' You must realize that I'm more than the sum of my lists! I guess I do play it too safe. I need to experiment a little more and not try so hard to control everything."

"I don't see myself as a model Learner, but I do use a lot of coping techniques," Carole modestly contributed. "And I do seem able to be situational in drawing on my resources and learning from my crises. . . . Well, maybe I'm a Learner. I wouldn't say I prefer any one style over the others. It may take the whole kit and caboodle to get me through my burnout."

"I still love the stories of other women's lives." mused Diana, "but you've got a point about me. I'm overly emotional. What's more, I've got to get organized! I've learned some new approaches to try . . . if I don't lose the notes I made."

Elinor called between vendor visits. "I can see how my Leaper style adds to my chaos. I need to pause, get the facts, and go over my options before leaping to conclusions." She quickly changed the subject. "I loved what everyone was wearing—send them in for some remedial work! Maybe we can barter skills and help each other?"

Exactly. If you've thought of friends, ex-bosses and lovers as you've read about each style, you can begin to understand them in a new way. These insights will also help you as you look at key areas of your life we'll consider in later chapters—your career, your relationships, your health. Meanwhile, we'll look at specific steps and resources to help you cope with change no matter *what* your style is.

CHAPTER III

Tapping Your Resources

WHETHER you see life as a game, an adventure, a story or something quite different, you now have a sense of how your history, your style and the key issues of your life interact with your ambitions. Next we'll look at building your coping resources to manage your life changes, in even the toughest of times, more effectively.

STEPS TO TAKE IN A CRISIS

Scientists keep telling us more about how our brains deal with complex problems. We develop and use models, we anticipate results. We bring our analytic and our intuitive modes together. We link various things and interpret the total picture. We predict, imagine, rehearse, test and process information that comes through our senses to solve problems and reach decisions.

Our brains are marvelously complex. We really are capable of handling many things. Then why are we so confused when a crisis hits? It helps—especially in a whirlwind of Domino change—to be clearer about what we're asking our brains to do. Instead of trying to grapple with everything at once and overwhelming our capacities, we can break things down into manageable, Discrete chunks. Even before we can picture the outcome we want, we can start moving in the direction we want to go, step by step.

These steps grew out of my research. I asked women what they did during periods of crisis and kept track of their responses. Since then, I've used these steps in helping the many people I've counseled. All five are essential to successful coping.

Let's look at them one at a time.

1. Change Your Perspective
2. Regain Control
3. Solve the Problems
4. Gain Support
5. Build Self-Esteem

You won't necessarily perform them in this sequence. You might, for example, gain support by calling a friend first. But do use all five. You'll notice that each relates to one of the five coping styles. Certain ones will seem more natural to you than others. Be sure not to skip the ones that are like the behaviors you normally avoid. By "stretching," you'll make progress, you'll learn more and you'll probably speed up your results.

Change Your Perspective

One of the most effective strategies in dealing with change is to alter the way you look at what happens. There's always more than one side to a story, more than one angle for viewing a major change. Instead of seeing only disaster or loss, try to see the challenge, the possibilities and, in fact, the opportunities. What's gone may be worth mourning, but what's ahead, though still unknown, is worth going after too.

When people first come to me after losing their jobs, they feel angry, betrayed or depressed. As we talk, they almost always admit they've been unhappy for some time yet didn't have the guts to quit. Eventually they're likely to say, "The company did me a favor. I'm much happier since leaving," or "Losing my job was the best thing that ever happened to me!"

Carol Hyatt and Linda Gottlieb in *When Smart People Fail* write of people "reinventing" themselves after a disaster, seeing themselves in a new light and finding the courage to do things they couldn't do before. **Changing perspective not only diminishes the pain, it can propel you onward to something better than what you left behind.**

Because it's easier said than done, here are some immediate steps to help you shift your perspective:

1. Create a space between the event and when you have to think of it again. Go to a movie, or do something relaxing at home such as listening to tapes or music or simply daydreaming. Be good to yourself.

2. Ask, "What can I learn from this experience?" As I mentioned earlier, major changes provide a great opportunity to learn about ourselves, to mature, examine our assumptions and add another notch on our belts on the way to wisdom. Keep a journal of your thoughts to look back on what you learned.

3. See the big picture. Looking at your situation from a distance, ask yourself, is this really such a big deal? As human suffering goes, is your crisis really among the worst things that could happen?

4. Tell yourself, "This too shall pass." Focus on your future. Imagine yourself beyond this immediate situation, six months, a year, five years from now, looking back on it. Look for the positive outcomes you'd like.

5. Regard the event as a "rite of passage" in your journey through life, as though you are being tested and will come out stronger. Try looking at your situation in a religious or spiritual context where your crisis is simply part of a larger plan for your life.

6. Know that there *are* choices, even now. You *can* take control of your life, once you're ready. See this time as a special time for assessing where you are and what you want for the future, a time to delve deeper into the meaning of your life and adjust your ambitions.

Among our five friends, Elinor, the Leaper, had extraordinary skills at changing perspective. Even when a new perspective wasn't called for, her attention would dart about, zooming in from new angles. She described her biggest crisis to date, losing her job: "It was like losing everything important. The ground was shifting beneath my feet." Before taking any positive steps, she questioned many of her assumptions, even asking herself if this was the career she really wanted. She decided that it was and that New York was where she wanted to be.

Eventually she reached out to her brother, with whom she hadn't spoken in years, and to her parents, who offered to lend her money to move back to New York. "It really took the edge off my desperation. I saw myself as connected to my family for the first time in a long time." Her panic vanished. She knew she wasn't alone and that there were options.

When you need to alter your perspective, draw on your own Leaper abilities. If you have a hobby that brings out your creative abilities, this is the time for it. Or, if you aren't at ease using Leaper skills yet, seek out a friend who has them. A multimodal approach will help you see your situation and your options in new, creative ways.

Regain Control

If your actions seem to have little impact on what happens to you, you're feeling a loss of control. Maybe your crisis is something you didn't ask for or a total surprise. Maybe it threatens your sense of security or even your concept of who you are. What you are undergoing can be downright scary. To protect yourself, you may act more like a Lister for a while, not taking risks. If you give in to the lack of control, you'll just spin your wheels as Elinor did, randomly opening her Rolodex, dialing old numbers, wrong numbers and everything but the right numbers.

Watch out for denial too. "But he can't be seeing someone else," a woman says, looking at the empty pillow at 2 A.M. People ignore the rumblings of a corporate shakeup, telling themselves they couldn't possibly be let go after their twenty loyal years. Bad things happen to nice people. Pretending your crisis isn't happening only delays the pain and the process that will help you get on with your life.

Then there's the impulse to pull the covers up around your ears, letting your mind mull over what happened as the hours go by. Depression leads to inactivity and slows down your progress too. If you sense yourself becoming depressed, go back to step one, create more space between you and the event. If you're sinking still deeper, get help from friends, a therapist or a doctor.

Here are some ways of controlling your emotions by yourself.

1. Practice "thought catching," a technique from cognitive therapy. Stop and hear how you magnify and exaggerate events. When you're thinking, "This is terrible," ask yourself, "Is this really a disaster—like the *Challenger* explosion? Or is it rather that I *prefer* it hadn't happened and, yes, I can deal with it." Diana found this technique helpful in dealing with her surgery. She'd been catastrophizing. She learned she was a strong, capable woman who had coped before.

2. Get a grip on your fear. Fear produces a whole symphony of biochemical reactions from our early "fight or flight" brain. We overreact, behaving as though a tiger were about to lunge and eat us alive. Practice breathing deeply, counting to ten or saying a prayer. This can do

wonders for you, actually altering your body's reactions. Get medical help if your anxiety doesn't ease up.

3. Talk it out. Find a good Listener who'll hear what you have to say and empathize. More later on friends.

4. Express any anger you feel in an acceptable way: hitting tennis balls, punching a pillow or singing a "mad" song from your favorite opera. Or let others express their anger at your situation. Your best friend or spouse may be furious over your being fired, betrayed or ripped off. Let them get angry, saving your energy to use on your own behalf.

5. Make a list. **Organize your thoughts and the things you know you must do by making a "to-do" list of people to call, things that need doing, the complete sequence of actions to take.** Like the Lister, anyone in a crisis can take comfort in giving structure to chaos. Then there's the satisfaction of crossing off each thing you accomplish.

6. Savor whatever joy or peace you may feel. Smell the flowers someone sends to your bedside, enjoy the surprise phone call from a friend or the job offer you weren't expecting. Relish little things: clean sheets, chicken soup, Mozart, stretching in the morning. Even in the worst of times, some things are still wonderful.

7. Read and collect information from books, pamphlets or magazine articles that can help you through your specific crisis. No matter what you're going through, even a rare disease, others have been there and know more. Find out all you can.

Solve the Problems

After you gather information, analyze the data. Discrete changes are particularly amenable to a problem-solving approach. Basically, this means analyzing what needs to be done. If you're in a Domino change, get help from a Logical friend to help you break things down and analyze the best course of action. A Lister can help you set goals and timetables, and can nudge you along too.

When Allison was younger, she left the Northeast for two years to live in Houston when Keith was transferred there. Planning a move with kids and a career was no easy feat. Here's how she did it:

1. She identified the factors pushing against a change (extra work load, leaving roots) and those pulling her toward it (advancement, possi-

ble pay raise, valuable experience). She analyzed how she might alter each barrier keeping her from changing.

2. She weighed all the variables (time, cost, disruption) of one course of action against others she might take, then decided which made the best combination.

3. She anticipated new problems that might arise from each action. She looked at the ramifications of the relocation on every aspect of her family's lives and the probabilities that "x" would occur if she did "y."

4. She used her computer for logistics—who moves at what time by what mode of transportation, her criteria for the kids' schools and affordable housing, renting out their New Jersey home, all her alternatives. Today she could tap relocation resources, but none were available to her then except what the van lines offered.

5. She prioritized tasks in the order they needed to be done, decided what was needed at each stage of the move (a garage sale, transferring the kids' records, preparing for movers).

6. After sorting through these steps, she stated her objectives, contingency plans and target dates best fitting her family's needs. She also arranged for a transfer to her company's field offices in Houston.

You may not need to be as thorough in your planning. However, elements of Allison's problem-solving are helpful in getting through any sort of change—a wedding, a maternity leave, switching jobs.

Gain Support

Why try to do something alone when you can easily get assistance and end up with better results? My clients confess they wish they'd asked for help sooner from their family and friends. Whether you need someone to open doors, give advice, temper your mood swings or lend you money, other people can help. You may be surprised at who comes through for you and who doesn't. You may find you've had some "fair-weather friends" who are afraid to get too close to someone else's disaster. Keep your spirits up and stick with the people who make it easy for you to do just that.

Women, especially Leapers and Listeners, who have a whole range of friends and acquaintances are more likely to reach out to others. Networks, friends and family can all make a difference. Women with Discrete changes may not fully understand the need for people in their lives until a personal crisis hits. Beth was fortunate to have friends when facing her divorce and her move. Many men, however, suffer through a divorce, a job loss or other difficult transition without ever confiding in or asking help from another human being.

Build Self-Esteem

More fragile than we'd like to acknowledge, self-esteem is often under-mined by events leading up to a marital breakup, a job loss or financial problems. People who come to me for outplacement counseling have sometimes undergone months of demoralizing treatment before receiving their pink slips. Impossible assignments, unrealistic deadlines, criticism at every turn.

"Why didn't I bail out sooner?" they ask. "What made me stay there and take it?" Dysfunctional offices and dysfunctional personal relation-ships have a very similar effect: They leave a person's self-esteem in need of repair and nurturing.

Carole overcame hurdles in her work life that might have weakened someone else. When upheaval swept her personal life, however, her self-esteem was threatened. She'd sensed something was wrong in her rela-tionship with Malcolm. After two passionate years with her, her live-in lover began to spend more time away from their apartment. "He always had excuses. His food products territory expanded, which meant traveling all over the Northeast. So when he told me he was spending the night in Boston, I bought it. It never occurred to me to check up on him. . . .

"Well, that's not really true. Something made me suspicious. Some odd phone calls where he'd listen more than talk, a change in the cologne he wore, a distancing that I thought meant he was worried about work. A few times too, he was out late without letting me know. We were both working hard and I'd try to remember if he'd told me he'd be away. One evening I'd made a special dinner with candles and no Malcolm!"

She finally confronted him. He apologized for not having said some-thing sooner. He was very fond of her, but the truth was very hard to talk about. "I asked him, 'What are you trying to tell me?' I was all ready to hear about another woman he was in love with. He said 'Sit down,' and he told me that he was gay and yes, there was someone else, a man. They'd just met. Before that there were other men, the whole time we'd been living together. I said, 'Get your ass out of here!' and I threw him out bag and baggage. I was like a mad woman."

Once he was gone she broke down and cried. The next day she called in sick, then called her closest friends. One arrived at the door with out-of-season raspberries and chocolate mousse. Another brought some "healing music" and a book of poems. Some just gave her time and hugs, as much as she needed.

"I felt he'd used and abused me. All that deception! I'd think back to some tender moment and realize that he hadn't been a hundred percent there with me. My whole romance was fake, a pretense! It was the ultimate betrayal. And how could I *not* have guessed?

"I decided he'd been trying to prove that he wasn't gay. Living with me had helped him decide that he was! There was no way I could look at this and feel good about myself. My femininity was being rejected.

"It was only later I realized I might have contracted AIDS. I had the test, of course, which was negative. But my God, he knowingly endangered my life. . . ."

Her therapist helped her separate it out, so that she realized Malcolm's problems were, in fact, Malcolm's problems and not hers. She read about bisexual men and homosexual men and about women who loved them. But mostly, she focused on herself and rebuilding her self-esteem. Her therapist provided some positive affirmations for her to repeat over and over: "I am strong. I am good. I am powerful. I am sexy."

"I said them in front of the mirror, at the gym while I rode the exercise bike, every time I wasn't busy. I was very good to myself. Got my hair styled, had a hot bubble bath every night, bought some new clothes. I'd have gone home to Chicago and cried on Mama's shoulder, but I'd already lost her too. That's why it was doubly hard. I got out the old photo album and reminded myself of where I'd come from and how far I'd really gone.

"But it takes time getting over a blow like that. I haven't had too many dates and I keep looking at men—'Is he or isn't he?' But at least I know I'm okay really. One morning I woke up and realized, *I'm going to make it*! No, it wasn't all smooth sailing after that, but the worst was over. It hadn't killed me. It made me stronger."

Although she might have gotten by with the help of friends, therapy can speed up the recovery process after a crisis of this magnitude. Some people find they've built a "front" that has to be examined before they can construct a firm foundation for their self-esteem. One thing is certain, other people—even strangers—pick up on a damaged self-image, making matters worse. Carole knew that at her lowest point she was not in the right state of mind for changing jobs.

She put all five coping styles into play and saw her crisis as an opportunity to learn too. **As you may be aware by now, you've been taking these steps as you read, for this whole book is designed to help you change your perspective, regain control and complete the other steps.**

Taking these five steps and using a broad range of coping skills can see you through really difficult times. It's like arming yourself for battle; you need every available weapon in your arsenal.

You'll also have an opportunity to review what you're missing in *Your Coping Resource Matrix* at the end of this chapter. Meanwhile, let's look into the resources professional women find helpful. You may find some you've overlooked.

COPING RESOURCES

I often ask women, "What resources did you find helpful in navigating your major life changes?" No two women were alike in their responses; the variety was truly amazing. With the exception of self-assessment and reading, most of the resources involved interaction with other people! They were, in order of frequency mentioned: friends, networks and professional organizations, role models, therapy, courses, family, bosses/ mentors and work colleagues.

Professional women's lists differ from those of women reentering the job market after a lengthy absence, who didn't have such a broad range of contacts, and from those of men, who depend less on other people altogether.

Friends

Friends are very important to professional women, who are more likely to be single or divorced and perhaps also living far from their families. Who is a friend? "Someone you can say anything to," "Someone who doesn't judge you," "Someone who'll let you get things off your chest" was how women described them. (Work colleagues might also be friends, but I've placed them in a different category and many professional women think of them differently.)

Friends who'd been through similar events were particularly helpful. In a work crisis, friends in the same industry would sometimes open doors or set up interviews. Certain friends helped with tasks such as shopping, résumé writing or finding an apartment. Some had lent money, provided a place to stay or a car to use.

Logicals and Listers get by with only a few friends outside of work, while Listeners and Leapers in the midst of Domino changes might call on *many* friends, each serving a different function. Listeners and Leapers are also more likely to join support groups with others wrestling with similar problems. In general, since more of their changes are personal, they call on people they know outside their places of work. Often those friends are the same individuals even as time passes and roles change. Some women mention having a particularly close friend with whom they really "let their hair down." Invited or not, such a friend manages to be there when you face surgery or get fired or have man problems.

At the time of her divorce, Beth had such a friend who opened her home and took her in. "She made me feel like a member of the family. I needed to finish out the semester before I could make my move to New York, but I couldn't spend another night with my alcoholic husband. Of course, anybody who takes in the wife of a violent alcoholic is taking a risk too. We kept him from finding out where I was."

Elinor had a good friend too, when she needed a couch for crashing and a sympathetic ear during her job search. "If I'd only stopped to think about the few good friends I have when the world went topsy-turvy," she said.

Friends, of course, are important to reentry women too, particularly displaced homemakers and divorcées. Many of these women lack the wide range of friends that professional women have made in their world of customers, suppliers and professional organizations. Professional women have the opportunity to make many friends *if* they work at it.

Beth, after leaving Roanoke for New York, linked up with a core of Virginians through friends of friends. She has remained close to some of them ever since then, besides finding many other friends through work, church and hobbies.

Women don't need to be told to make friends. But a woman with a problem may need to be reminded to pick up the phone and call one of them. Some still worry about "burdening" others with their problems. More often, friends are hurt if not at least informed of a crisis or a situation where they might help.

Family

Women with Domino changes are more likely to mention supportive family members—mothers, husbands, sisters. How a husband acts in a crisis is very important. One woman deliberately did not tell her husband until after her exploratory surgery. "It would have been a personal crisis for him and he's more likely to panic at such times than I am. I didn't think I could handle that." One about to lose her job found that telling her husband was one of the most difficult things she had to do.

More women, however, had husbands who were caring and genuinely helpful, as Diana's was. A mate whose coping style complements yours will bring some essential skills to the problem as Nate did in insisting on the facts.

Family members, more than other people, can be nonjudgmental, enabling the professional woman to step down from the tightrope, be herself and let her emotions pour out, if necessary. It doesn't matter that they don't understand the demands or the structure of the world you've chosen for your career. Allison's mother had always been her greatest fan, although she couldn't imagine why a lawyer wasn't handling divorce cases, nor did she understand Allison's ultimate ambition. "What is a corporate secretary, dear?" she asked.

It can take courage to call a family member, especially after contact has been broken. For Elinor, it took desperation, but she swallowed her pride and made long-distance calls to her parents and her brother.

Friends and family are key in your steps to recovery. Keep the channels of communication open, if you can. Be careful, though, not to wear out your welcome by asking for favors too often.

Networks

Every woman in the working world has the beginnings of a network. Build yours by collecting business cards and keeping your address book or Rolodex current. Drop a note to individuals you've especially enjoyed meeting. It's not good to call others in your network only when you need them. Most networkers expect quid pro quo. Be a magnet for information worth sharing, say, about available apartments or job openings. Never miss a chance to do somebody a small favor, and write brief "thank you" notes when someone does one for you.

An effective network can take years to grow and needs to be carefully tended. People forget you and may assume you've moved if they don't hear from you in a while. Listeners are good networkers, but so are most other women with some experience.

Networkers have mastered the art of the quick phone call that accomplishes a lot. Sometimes more time is needed. It's not unusual for a woman to ask, "Can I get back to you later?" and if the topic warrants a lengthy discussion, set a time for a longer call.

Networks can ease relocation and make business travel more interesting. Arriving in Houston, Allison made one phone call and was invited to a congenial group of professional women who made her stay there far more pleasant. Beth, attending conventions in Atlanta, Denver and other cities, would get away from the hotel one evening to be with a member of her nationwide network.

Networks are invaluable when you're searching for a new job or launching a new business. Also, many women report receiving help from their networks in personal dilemmas involving child care, coping problems with teenagers and aging parents. Whatever is at stake, your networks can often expand your options.

Role Models

A role model is somebody usually a little older and wiser who has already attained what you aspire to, professionally, personally, even spiritually. When there's no one nearby, a famous person or even a fictional character can help you imagine how you could be and serve to crystalize your ambitions.

Besides older role models, women look to peers who've already had similar experiences. The peer model helps you realize "if she can do it, I can," and may offer suggestions for weathering a crisis. Peer models can also boost your confidence in yourself when you need to get up and going.

Allison eventually went to a support group where she got firsthand help from parents of teenagers with drug problems. Beth went to Al-Anon, the twelve-step program for friends and family members of alcoholics and addicts. In both instances, peer models helped.

Bosses/Mentors

Mentors and bosses who act as mentors are crucial to career progress. Studies show that the majority of executives had more than one mentor, and that they learned something, however painfully, from bad bosses. Interestingly, *only* individuals who are secure in their work cite bosses and mentors among their helpful resources.

To be effective, a mentor must have reached a high enough level to have influence to use in your favor. Often they may be men who aren't prejudiced against women. On the contrary, they believe that you have the potential to go far. They're older and more astute about your field and its internal politics. They may recommend you for new assignments, promotions and raises, helping you gain acceptance at progressively higher levels. They may also push you in new directions, stimulate you creatively and give you constructive feedback. Yet you might not even be aware that you are currently being mentored.

If you want a mentor, you have to work at getting one. Carole actively sought mentoring from her bosses, many of whom have been women. She went out of her way to make them look good, delivered beyond their expectations and matched their "chemistry" or style. She asked for their career advice but not their assistance with personal matters. "My boss was very kind when my mother died and I needed some time away. I also missed a week's work when I broke up with Malcolm, but everybody at work thought I was out with the flu. It's better that way, not airing a lot of problems at the office." She walked a fine line.

Women at the Domino end of the Continuum, who see the boss as the "enemy," derive less of this sort of help. Leaving large corporations to "go it alone," they usually lack the benefit of mentors to point the way. Entrepreneurial women find other sources of support, relying on different people—accountants, investors, etc. However, a good relationship with a former boss often enables a woman to later consult to the company she's left.

What about bad bosses? Some are truly toxic, taking credit for your work, playing favorites, second-guessing your decisions. Allison's former boss, refusing to acknowledge her ambitions, couldn't understand her wanting to continue working after her son was born. Elinor, who felt the absence of boss-mentors, might have floundered less with seasoned advice from veterans of the store wars. Even bad bosses might surprise you with excellent references, and in retrospect, you may find you have learned something from them, if only how *not* to supervise.

Work Colleagues

Individuals near your level help create a pleasant and productive working environment. They can share information, especially the "inside" information that's hard to come by. They can also cover for you when you have a heavy work load or need time off. They provide a different perspective on what's going on at work—why the boss is behaving differently, how successful a meeting was, how to handle a subordinate. The camaraderie of a good team enhances productivity as almost nothing else can.

For some women, work colleagues are like extended family. Diana found "family" wherever she went. But there are also those who become too involved with work colleagues, playing out family-like drama that doesn't belong in the workplace, becoming jealous or too easily hurt, for example. The smartest of work colleagues share the most when they're no longer both working for the same company. Logical and Lister women are very careful about what they reveal at work. They fear that intimate details of their lives could endanger their corporate images, or could be used against them by the unscrupulous. At any level you may find people whose only concern is furthering their own interests and who will do so at the expense of others. Watch out for them, especially if you tend to be too trusting.

Professional Associations

The Financial Women's Association, American Society of Training and Development, Women in Communication and American Psychological Association are just a few professional associations. Whatever your field is, it probably has a group you could join. In small towns, you'll find Toastmasters and the Chamber of Commerce. If you're lucky, your employer pays for your membership and perhaps even bears the expense for you to attend regional or national conventions.

All of these groups exist to help your career or your business. Some have expert speakers, special seminars and opportunities for training, some offer referral services and business leads. They may have information banks useful to newcomers to the field or to those teaching others about the profession.

If you have a choice of several groups, you could join as many as you have time for. Some women belong to four or five. You could select one or two that seem worthwhile. Before deciding, attend meetings as a guest, and ask about the benefits. Also, ask yourself if you feel comfortable among these people and if belonging will make a difference in your career. Just joining may not be enough, however. Volunteering for local committees helps people see what you can do; being active at the regional or national level gives you considerable visibility in your field.

Professional associations often provide the most fruitful job leads; you'll hear of openings in your field even before they're advertised. As an insider, you're privy to all sorts of information, such as what job moves will look best on your résumé and what companies offer the best benefits or child-care programs. Should you relocate, a national organization can refer you to a chapter in your new area and even help you with job leads there.

Such extensive resources aren't usually open to reentry women. Often you must be already working in the field before you can join an organization, and you may need a minimum number of years and a sponsor as well.

As people advance in their fields, they may form smaller groups of colleagues whose discussions meet their more sophisticated needs. They rarely attend the larger group meetings and then only to give a speech or receive an award. Allison doesn't go to her Bar Association's local meetings, but belongs to a small group of women attorneys active in environmental issues.

Beth was active in organizations serving the training industry and attended annual conferences on her specialty, technical training. When restructuring threatened her spot in her company, she felt fortunate to have made many contacts. "I know people I might work for—or with. I think change is in the wind at my company and I want to be ready." As a Lister, she was especially methodical in pinning down details.

Carole found that with several personal and professional networks as well as professional organizations, she was becoming "grouped out." However, she commented on the groups she found most helpful. "I met one kind of woman at my Business and Professional Women's Club. Their members couldn't be more helpful or gracious. It's a very nurturing group that also offers leadership training. The National Association of Bank Women gave me specific training in leadership and presentation skills plus a chance to meet women from banks all over the country." She also showed me plaques she was awarded for service.

Diana would have liked belonging to a lot of groups, but limited her activities to have time for her family and herself. She liked the star speakers at Women in Communication, the interchange with corporate counterparts in the International Association of Business Communicators and the less formal monthly dinner meetings of a small group of cosmetics industry women. Each group met different Listener needs for her.

Courses

No category of resources professional women use is more diverse. This includes not only academic courses, but workshops on such topics as executive leadership, mid-life, career development, writing, public speaking, design, photography, running a small business, philosophy and personal growth. Under personal growth, women in my original sample listed mind-expanding marathon weekends, seminars, retreats and psychological group trainings.

Many women take courses in new fields they plan to enter. As she planned her move, Beth took workshops on consulting skills, marketing and opening a small business. Others take courses to learn and test new skills that they hope to apply professionally such as public speaking, writing and computer technology. Some take courses to develop hobbies, ease stress, solve personal problems and meet new people.

The women I questioned liked the course formats offered by professional organizations, institutions offering continuing education and personal growth experts. Those in the midst of Domino changes seemed to prefer less formal, more experiential courses that stimulated their imagination in group settings. These women chose topics pertaining to their *whole* life, not just their careers. They found the support of others with similar problems helpful. They also maintained that the structure of a course as opposed to self-directed work kept them on track.

Those dealing with Discrete changes took very few courses. They preferred panels of senior people in their fields, seminars or programs by business alumni clubs on business topics like negotiating, time management, corporate games and politics, business writing and presentation skills. They wanted more structure, more how-to specifics, more advice on trade-offs, feedback—in short, content related to careers, with question-and-answer periods. In general, they wanted specific help with specific problems rather than the more general life planning or personal-growth programs to which the other group was drawn.

As you become familiar with the different coping styles, these preferences make sense. Leapers and Listeners, who enjoy the arts, music and writing, are more in tune with experiential processes. Elinor would sign up for a self-improvement course if it promised changes that fit her picture of how she'd like to be. Diana would enroll in a course with a powerful and interesting teacher or guru. If something "felt right," they'd be willing to get involved without knowing just where it was going. They didn't demand to know what would be covered or what the specific results would be.

Listers and Logicals perceive more value in a practical, cognitive, task-related approach. They enroll in courses to solve specific "discrete" problems. They want to know in advance the content of the course and its benefits. They also like working with checklists, references for further study and an agenda for each session. Learners respond well to either type of experience.

Trying New Age techniques for creative writing, Diana was turned on by the mix of music, guided imagery, role playing, chanting, physical movement, art and dream analysis. It opened up parts of her she hadn't known existed. Carole said of a similar experience, "It blew my mind!" She also explained how it was analogous to brainstorming, then listed some specific benefits to her life and her career. Ever the Learner, Carole could probably sell Listers and Logicals on New Age courses: She'd explain how they work and spell out the concrete benefits.

Reading

Self-directed help through reading was mentioned more often by women under forty. Certainly, *all* women read to stay abreast in their fields, but younger women do more reading and take more courses specifically to help them through career changes and other transitions. Perhaps older professional women are more settled in their careers and feel more confident about their coping abilities. However, many women over forty do make career changes.

As publishers know, contemporary women, who lead multifaceted lives, buy many types of books. Men buy far fewer self-help books, perhaps for the same reasons they are less likely to seek counseling or join support groups. It may be they don't see themselves as needing help or they don't want to be perceived as needing help.

If you'd like to read further on any of the topics in this book, see the "Additional Resources" section, organized by chapter topics. Although a bookstore or library might not be the first place you head in a crisis, plenty of help is waiting for you there.

Self-Assessment

Spending time alone reflecting can be helpful in sorting out who you are and what you want. This is what I mean by self-assessment. It entails an analysis of your patterns, values, interests and skills. It combines aspects of reading, tests, exercises, courses and workshops, and it includes insights outside of therapy sessions.

In completing exercises and tests such as the ones in this book, you can address your life issues and emotions. You may choose specific ideas to mull over and contemplate in greater depth. Ultimately, you may alter how you view yourself and your world through the insights you gain. To people in Domino changes, this is an ongoing process; for those in Discrete changes, a task to be completed.

Therapy

Initially I'd been concerned to find that forty-eight percent of the women in my original sample had used therapy in coping with major changes. Psychologists I asked assured me that this is not an unusual percentage among high-achieving, well-paid, highly educated urban professional women. Apparently they see therapy as another useful resource, certainly not something to be ashamed of or to avoid mentioning in an interview.

The women with Domino changes experienced more incidents that would lead them to seek therapy. Listeners and Leapers may prefer traditional psychotherapy, perhaps with a psychoanalytical orientation for an in-depth examination of childhood and unconscious issues, to understand their emotions better. After realizing that she had projected her parents onto her therapist, Elinor learned that some of her present-day reactions were inappropriate. New Age or humanistic workshops hold an appeal for most Listeners and Leapers too. Elinor wholly believed in art and music therapy, and in neurolinguistic programming. She thrived on using her imagination, and, as she said, "I love when those light bulbs go on!"

Diana hadn't been in therapy, but her journal-writing workshop served much the same purpose. "My emotions are there for all to see and if I can't understand them, my friends help me," she said.

Carole's therapy after Malcolm's betrayal was interpersonal. "I wanted to understand this faulty relationship and get some help dealing with my depression. I'm open to New Age workshops too. I'm energized and in a different place after one."

Logicals and Listers want practical, short-term goal-directed behavioral and cognitive therapies. For example, Beth, who went to Al-Anon, also used cognitive therapy in adjusting to her new relationship. It helped her deal with the here and now, and routinely gave her homework.

Allison's family was deeply grateful for the family therapy that helped address Scotty's drug problem. She said, "I was doing everything wrong. You need to see how you're contributing to the problem."

Virtually all the comments I heard on therapy were positive, whether therapy was short-term or extended. Women who have spent years in therapy felt this was what they needed. Those who've used it on a short-term basis to deal with specific conflicts or crises are also likely to recommend their therapists to friends as they would any other resource.

Stress Reducers

Beyond these resources and those offered by employers, there are four other categories of resources that can help in dealing with the stress that can accompany major life changes.

Men often consider sports a vital resource, and women are now discovering the importance of physical stress reducers. Women I interviewed frequently mentioned jogging, walking, swimming, health-club classes, dance, biofeedback and massage. Some gave golf, tennis or another sport top priority.

A second group of resources is spiritual. These might include meditation, prayer, religious services or whatever your beliefs call for. They can give you a sense of peace, of calm in a crisis, a view of a larger purpose to everything.

You might plan a weekend or a vacation at a religious or spiritual retreat. You might also spend a Saturday afternoon in the country outdoors or in front of a fireplace. Or curl up in a city apartment among pillows with your favorite music playing softly. If you can find a setting that relaxes you—only for a little while—the process of self-discovery can begin. Listen to those inner voices that you may have suppressed. They may have something to say about the future you're planning.

Aesthetic resources can go hand in hand with spiritual ones, or they may appeal to people who'd prefer to skip the spiritual. Do something creative—painting, singing, writing poetry, playing music or acting in a play to wake up your Leaper abilities. Creative activities can be useful too, when you're incubating new ideas. These activities use a different part of your brain and sometimes counterbalance negative feelings that might have stuck in your consciousness. Creating something can also yield personal satisfaction at a time when other elements of your life are in jeopardy.

Then there are escapes—reading novels, going to movies, watching TV, playing cards. Since you probably don't have time for many escapes, pick the ones you really enjoy. Have some fun. Take a break of a few hours. It can give you pleasure in the midst of pain and can also help create that space you need between yourself and your crisis. Escapes are fine as long as you don't let them drag you into lethargy.

Some things are definitely *not* helpful:

1. Books that make you feel deficient.
2. Pollyannas with "shoulds."
3. Insensitive bosses, family or friends.
4. Executive searchers who undermine your confidence.
5. "Quick-fix" remedies.
6. Relying solely on yourself when effective resources are everywhere.
7. Feeling sorry for yourself.
8. Dreaming of revenge.
9. Postponing dealing with problems that you *can* do something about.

Your problems demand your focus, usually the sooner the better. They won't go away by themselves. But remember too, *not* deciding is a form of decision. **Be sure you've attacked the problem with all of your styles before opting not to act.** Inactivity can be an informed choice, as in the case of waiting to be terminated to take advantage of the severance package after weighing the odds and considering the options.

Whether you're open and candid or reserved will determine what resources you seek. Women with Domino changes favored intimate resources such as family and therapy. Those with Discrete problems relied upon the less intimate resources: bosses, work colleagues and reading.

Professional women are quite casual in selecting the resources they use. Those undergoing Domino episodes are apt to go to friends not only for support but for advice on choosing therapists, classes or groups. Typically, a woman might say that a particular resource helped others she knew, so she decided to try it. Or it was recommended by someone she respected. Often too, women choose a source of help because "it feels right." Women in a Discrete change usually seek a resource that matches their specific problem.

When the crisis is over, women who've sought and used a resource of one kind or another are almost always pleased with the help they got. One said *everything* she tried was helpful. All of the women I've asked recall many more resources that are helpful than ones that were not.

This indicates a positive, upbeat attitude toward what's available, also perhaps gratitude for help that was given. The better we understand ourselves and the clearer our future goals are, however, the better we can select resources that will be catalysts in attaining our goals.

As a working woman today, you may have many frustrations and problems. You may have hit a glass ceiling in your career, you may be alone without a "significant other" in your life or you may be far away from your parents, siblings and the people you grew up with. Probably your life hasn't turned out as you'd once dreamed and some of your most cherished ambitions may seem to be thwarted. But simply because you are a woman alive and functioning here and now, you have an abundance of resources at your fingertips. Men may have more career advantages, but they don't use this wealth of resources as you can. Don't forget they're there.

To help you I've designed "Your Coping Resource Matrix." Across the top are the five steps to take to move you through a crisis. Down the left-hand column are the coping resources you can use to help you achieve those steps. In the example, you can see how Carole took the steps and used the resources in coping with her career burnout, her boyfriend's betrayal and her mother's death.

EXERCISE I

YOUR COPING RESOURCE MATRIX

CAROLE'S EXAMPLE

Instructions: On the next matrix (p. 86), check off the resources that might help you. (The check marks show how Carole assessed her needs. To change her perspective she used friends, role models, therapy and spiritual activities.)

YOUR COPING RESOURCE MATRIX

1. Instructions: Check off the coping resources for each of the five steps you need to take in getting through your current change. Write in specific names, organizations, courses and books for your action plan on the blank copy of the matrix on page 87.

Considerations: Does the change you are now experiencing call for more formal, more structured and less intimate problem-solving resources such as

Carole's Example

Transition Steps

Coping Resources	Change Your Perspective	Regain Control	Problem Solve	Gain Support	Build Self-Esteem	Other	Total
Friends	✔			✔	✔		
Family				✔	✔		
Role Models	✔			✔			
Therapy	✔			✔	✔		
Networks				✔			
Professional Organizations			✔	✔	✔		
Courses		✔	✔				
Reading		✔	✔				
Self-Assessment		✔			✔		
Bosses/Mentors		✔	✔	?			
Work Colleagues		✔	✔	?			
Stress Reducers Physical						✔	
Aesthetic						✔	
Spiritual	✔						
Escape						✔	
Other							
Total							

YOUR COPING
RESOURCE MATRIX

Transition Steps

Coping Resources	Change Your Perspective	Regain Control	Problem Solve	Gain Support	Build Self-Esteem	Other	Total
Friends							
Family							
Role Models							
Therapy							
Networks							
Professional Organizations							
Courses							
Reading							
Self-Assessment							
Bosses/Mentors							
Work Colleagues							
Stress Reducers Physical							
Aesthetic							
Spiritual							
Escape							
Other							
Total							

courses and books? Or do you need intimate, informal, unstructured support from friends, family and therapy to help with your feelings? Which of these resources are you using? Which are you avoiding? Which might you add to your coping repertoire?

2. Have you covered all five steps? What are the new resources you plan to incorporate in your coping repertoire? _____

_____

_____

3. If you haven't made a "to do" list after reading this chapter, now's the time. What can you do *right now* to improve or change your situation? ___

_____

_____

_____

What can you do by the end of the day? _____

_____

_____

By tomorrow? _____

_____

_____

For each day of this week? _____

_____

_____

Who can be your partner in helping you and keeping you on track? ___

_____

Go for it. NOW!

PROGRESS REPORT

As you become more of a Learner, you'll stretch into areas where you haven't ventured before. Here's how our friends fared with unfamiliar coping strategies.

"I know I'm not a Logical," Leaper Elinor concluded. "I found the section on problem solving new and, frankly, exciting. I hadn't really broken things down that way before. It's a technique that really gives me an edge!" Elinor found her brother helpful in questioning her alternatives and prioritizing what she needed to do. She started reading books for high-level executives and doing more financial research on target companies for her job campaign.

Diana, our Listener, needed to develop Lister skills. "I'm reading a book on time management that comes with a video. Also, I'm making 'to do' lists so I can be more specific about what chores need to be done. What's more, I realize my novel will be better if I take more care in structuring and outlining it."

As a Lister, Beth decided she needed Leaper help. "I brainstormed with friends, took a workshop on dreams and have tried to visualize myself in my next move." But, as we'll see, some Listener help in sizing up potential partners in her new venture might have been valuable too.

Logical Allison acknowledged needing Listener help. "Support groups of people with similar problems have helpful suggestions I'd have never thought of. It's good to know that I'm not all alone with either of these problems. Still, I get uncomfortable when total strangers burst into tears."

Carole, the Learner, integrated help from the four other coping styles to help her through her crisis. Logical analysis, lists, reaching out to friends and creative and New Age techniques all contributed to her recovery.

Your greatest resource in coping is you—your own brain, your own styles and your wealth of past experiences. Carole's mix might not be yours, but with a similar variety in your coping strategies, you can move through your present crisis and be well prepared for whatever may lie ahead. Remember, you've coped before.

Next we'll look at the key areas of your life, how they relate to each other and to your ambitions.

PART II

SHAPING

YOUR LIFE

The first part of the book provided a framework for getting beyond whatever specific changes or problems might be plaguing you and for handling future changes better. We've seen how developing our coping skills and competencies sharpens our effectiveness in a variety of situations, especially career challenges. Tapping into the many resources we have as working women helps us navigate the stormy seas that are sure to lie ahead no matter how carefully we map our route.

Today's and tomorrow's world demands that we be fluid in our planning, flexible in our expectations. Instead of drawing up a precise blueprint for our lives or our careers, we may find it more useful to *shape* our futures in a more general way, filling in the details as we go along.

Part II will examine ways we can shape the key areas of our lives: careers, relationships and health. Although we often think of ambitions as being career ambitions, women's hopes and aspirations for the future invariably involve other roles and relationships too. Health, of course, affects everything we hope for, although we're apt to take it for granted unless something goes wrong. We'll see too how our coping styles relate to career planning, making relationships work and staying healthy.

New Shapes in Careers

It's a brand-new era. Do you know where your career is?

You're far from alone if it has run aground or veered off unpredictably. You don't need to be reminded that recent trends have played havoc with even the best-laid five- and ten-year plans. It's still possible, however, to set ambitions for the future and find ways to attain them.

Earlier I called working women *pioneers*. Although many have been thrown into crisis by turbulence in the workplace, they've fanned the winds of change too. They've carved out new ways of working, and given new meaning and new shapes to the concept of careers. This chapter will trace traditional and new ways women's careers evolve. **It will also highlight specific pitfalls to watch for and planning strategies to help you avoid career casualties and chart the future you want.**

Defining Our Careers

Few people know early on what they want to be. Most of us have *many* possibilities, some more realistic than others. Some women expect to find something "perfect" that meshes with their abilities as nothing else can. Eventually reality sets in and we realize that no career is perfect, though some are better matches for our abilities than others.

So we adjust our expectations. We build skills, gain experience and develop a network. Once in a career that seems like a fit, we conform to the norms of that industry and that culture. In a few years we know whether it was a good match or not.

The women I've questioned in my research have worked in a variety of early jobs ranging from teacher to "Jill of all trades" in small companies. By the late seventies, though, they looked forward to Classic Career patterns; that is, spending a lifetime in the same field, moving steadily upward, working in one or perhaps two organizations. They worked harder and longer than their male colleagues. In a decade they expected to be near the top.

ALLISON'S CLASSIC CAREER

Allison typifies the woman who chose the Classic Career track. She had good grades in school and majored in biochemistry in college at Boston University. But there wasn't much future for women in science then, so she got a job in a law firm doing paralegal work and started taking law courses at night at Rutgers.

She studied law as it related to the energy industry, using her scientific studies to put together a specialty that would impress employers. She went from paralegal to administrative assistant—a step not required of her male peers. Later, as associate counsel, she worked on contracts, leases, licensing and minor litigation involving the company's service stations.

"The experience was invaluable in learning about the problems in that sector of our business, but it got boring after a while," she said. Asking for new assignments, she became involved with patent applications, trademarks and sale/leaseback agreements for other departments. "To be really valuable, I wanted my experience to have a broad scope, unlike my male colleagues, who didn't care if they were learning, but who were always bragging about their wins." She thought such bragging was a lot of "hot air" and that *she* was more serious, worked harder.

Finally at headquarters, she worked on employment contracts, compliance with trade regulations, insurance and damage claims, and served on teams with more senior attorneys (all male) for major litigation over drilling rights.

In 1978 her company had been restructured after the impact of the oil crisis, and was now pursuing natural gas and chemical production. It was also acquiring high-tech companies right and left. "I'm lucky to have survived in this industry," Allison said. "Only my field expertise and the cost of outside lawyers has saved me from the cutbacks. I haven't pushed for promotion. It's too risky."

By 1988 Allison was a senior attorney, having put in time with several spun-off subsidiaries, as well as serving on task forces and committees dealing with company personnel and environmental issues. Computers made the research and legal brief–writing part of her job easier and faster than when she used longhand, which some of her male colleagues still resorted to. Her career had been a series of logical moves, yet her goal of corporate secretary seemed as far away as it had been ten years earlier.

The reality, of course, is different from what Allison anticipated, as it is for many of the 1,200 high-level women I tracked as director of Catalyst's Corporate Board Resource. Our team built extensive files on high-achieving women—presidents of colleges, top corporate officers, women who ran and owned multimillion dollar businesses, executives of corporate-board caliber.

I worked with corporate chairmen, helping them select women meeting their criteria for their boards. I also worked with women in many major cities, helping them set up comparable resource banks for their local profit and not-for-profit boards.

Reviewing the backgrounds of these 1,200 women, I was struck by a difference in their careers. Unlike high-level men, very few high-level women in Catalyst's early eighties files had stayed with only one or two companies.

Those who had stayed were more narrow in their range of experience than the ones who had moved from company to company or sector to sector. Surprisingly, however, a woman with twenty-five years at company X, even as its highest level woman, impressed CEOs less than women who had been science or business professors and served as heads of multimillion-dollar government agencies or published important articles.

These women with varied experience offered CEOs something they didn't already have. They added a new perspective, asked pointed questions, were intellectually more challenging than women *or* men whose lack of broad experience left them less flexible and hampered by tunnel vision. It seemed that the CEOs were seeking Learners with broader or, at least, different perspectives, rather than Logicals with functional depth.

With a few exceptions, these women had held staff jobs or been powerful individual contributors with small staffs of their own. These conditions were typical of the seventies, and women succeeded in spite of them.

THE *NEW* CLASSIC CAREER

Technological, global and economic trends have altered the workplace, the shape of hierarchies and the ways business is conducted. Demographic and sociological trends have shifted our perspectives too. We want what is possible.

As a result, the corporate ladder and the classic up-the-ladder career path have taken new shapes. The upward thrust is much flatter, its individual steps take longer and are tougher to climb with *fewer* rungs.

THE CLASSIC CAREER

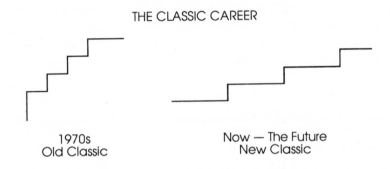

1970s
Old Classic

Now — The Future
New Classic

Many of the women I've tracked started on the Classic Career path. They were enthusiastic and hardworking, as people often are when offered new opportunities. They learned fast too, assimilating the corporate culture and gaining insight into the power structure.

Companies hired consultants in the eighties to help managers deal with the new multicultural work force, which now included women and minorities. Nevertheless, legions of them left.

Women lucky enough to have mentors, helpful colleagues and a better fit with their companies' culture hoped that paying their dues mattered after all. Most took staff jobs, following their interests to such departments as public relations or personnel, not recognizing that line experience with responsibility for profits is necessary to be seen as a "comer."

Some had their ambitions altered for *positive* reasons. Unexpected promotions, new opportunities and serendipitous occurrences gave them reason to aspire to greater goals than they'd initially set. Some, but not all, women chalk such surprises up to luck rather than to their own efforts. Those who believed they were in control of their careers gave twice as many positive reasons for altered ambitions as those who experienced Domino changes.

Seeing the light that filters down through the corporate hierarchy, some women campaigned for one to two years for lateral or lower-paid line positions to broaden their profit-generating experience. They moved to sales and paid their dues again, often managing a staff of mostly men, as they moved up a different track. Some asked for transfers to gain field experience and paid still more dues, often in isolation as the only single woman in a circle of married men.

They were well aware of the discrimination suits, attitude surveys and articles revealing how men felt about women bosses by now. Most didn't contemplate bringing suit themselves. They were determined to succeed *in spite of* the climate and the odds.

Then came the early eighties, the Reagan administration and the cutbacks at the Equal Employment Opportunity Commission. Advancement for women and minorities ground to a halt. Successive glass ceilings grew thicker. The hopes of many women were dashed and their loyalties betrayed. Even in 1990, articles reported these ceilings and women leaving corporations for "lack of opportunity," *not* just to have families. Single women leave too, to maximize the opportunities elsewhere.

Will the Classic Career survive for women? Yes, for some, at any rate. Fifty percent of corporate women surveyed (versus seventy-six percent of the men) by *U.S. News and World Report* in 1988 expected to stay with their large organizations. Fifty-six percent of the women (versus forty percent of the men) felt that shifting from company to company as opportunities arise was the way to get ahead. Having invested time and money in their skills and experience, they wanted the sophisticated resources of large companies in order to be at the cutting edge. But the means of advancing aren't the same now.

A woman may remain with one company for a decade, but now she may serve on more task forces, get continual training and work from home. She may be called an associate and may be permitted to create her own title as her male colleagues do. She may even drop out, start a business, then "recycle" her experience back to a large company.

What is different today is that innovation, creativity and multicultural sensitivity are rewarded. Jobs are more interesting, giving employees a greater sense of control and more autonomy as companies learn to motivate the new "knowledge" worker. **What's in your head counts, more**

than where that head is located geographically, or what hours it's accessible. Companies are discovering that if people are bored or frustrated or worried about children or aging parents at home, longer hours won't increase their productivity.

Studies on worker productivity and development that were based on mostly white males really aren't relevant anymore. Work isn't organized the same way it once was. Passive workers plateaued at mid-career aren't being kept on. Companies cut "deadwood," often brutally. Aggressive, flexible, forward-thinking workers with skills in *each* of the five styles are in demand.

Allison's reasons for staying on were mixed. "I wanted to learn as much as I could. I tried not to get pigeonholed into one narrow specialty. My last boss was responsive to my needs for challenge and growth. I even invited him home to dinner so we could demonstrate how Keith was linked to his company with our home computer in ways our company wasn't yet using. It took an effort, but I think he liked my ambition and hard work."

"But for me the glow has worn off," she said thoughtfully. "I once had visions of changing the world, making it better. Other lawyers I know are turning to public-interest law, helping the disadvantaged or working for environmental issues. I wish I could afford to do that."

Her family's budget, which now included her father's medical expenses and her daughter's university bills, permitted her very little leeway. Allison's salary went quickly. Unlike their younger friends, she and Keith always paid as they went and saved. They would have felt strapped without a nest egg and investments, though lately they'd been dipping into both.

"So many women are opting out. I guess we'd all hoped to change things more. Women are blocked from the top at so many companies. I know I'll never be corporate secretary at *this* company. That's an ambition I just have to let go of." She took a deep breath.

"Keith and I have talked about what's next in our lives," she said almost wistfully. "Of course, we have contingency plans. Doesn't everybody?"

Although she smiled, she seemed really concerned as she reached for her running shoes and battered briefcase. "Give me five years and I'll have something else in place—environmental work maybe. There's an enormous need there." The gleam returned to her eyes. As we went our separate ways, I saw her deftly weaving through the crowds in her company's lobby.

Allison chose to stick with her New Classic Career for the time being. It made logical sense at this stage of her life. Meanwhile other women are pioneering alternative career paths.

FOUR NEW SHAPES IN CAREERS

By 1985, only *one* of the women in my research who'd had Domino changes was still working for her original company. Nearly half had started their own small businesses. Several were home with small children and some had moved to different sectors of the economy: education, the arts and social agencies.

Of those few with Discrete changes who had left their original companies by 1985, one had moved to a company in another state, and three had their own businesses.

I hear from them now and then and they keep changing! **It's easy to see that each woman chooses her own path, alters her ambitions in ways satisfying to her.**

The most popular move for all workers on a national level is to self-employment in the service industry. This can be consulting, retail outlets, educational services, public relations, advertising, real estate sales and management. Over four million women now have their own small businesses. Over a third of U.S. businesses are owned by women, generating over $100 billion in revenues each year. One survey showed that nearly half of all working women *want* to start businesses.

Entrepreneurship doesn't suit everyone, of course. Some women go from their own businesses back to corporations. Others go from agency to agency, business to business, in and out of teaching.

To get a handle on these new career mixes, I went beyond my original research. Having tracked the careers of 1,200 women executives at Catalyst for five years and counseled some 1,500, I had lots of résumés and career histories to consider. I looked at lives over time, searching for patterns and themes.

Besides the New Classic, four other shapes in careers emerged. I call these Concentric, Concurrent, Combination and Contingency. They're the result of women (and some men) pioneering new life-styles. As you can see, each is easily represented by a symbol. Each has a place on the Change Continuum as follows:

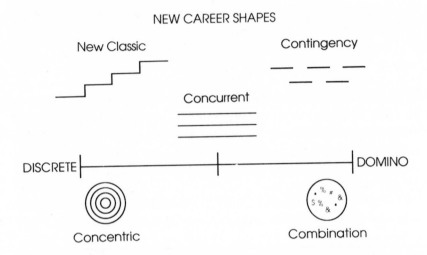

NEW CAREER SHAPES

Six and a half million people are currently unemployed. Another sixty-three million are not in the labor force, among them students, home-makers and volunteers. Over ten million are self-employed and another fifteen million work part-time. Classic Careers are becoming more the exception than the rule. Often too, they're not the goal either. Other shapes not only fit better in the rather tumultuous world most of us live in, but they suit our individual needs better too.

Concentric Careers

Concentric Careers look like bull's-eyes or umbrellas. You start out with a core of interests and career-specific expertise, then add successive layers to it, each enhancing the others, all relating synergistically. A Concentric Career might be a business of your own that you build around a central idea, under the umbrella of a particular interest.

Beth's career pattern became Concentric as she prepared to leave her job for a consulting career. "I've relished working in this company. We've been through so many changes here. I've added new skills and tested myself in new situations without too much risk."

Actually, she'd had two Classic Careers up to now. The first was brief, progressing from teaching assistant to instructor to assistant professor at her college in Roanoke. When she didn't get tenure, she decided to abandon academia.

"A friend told me about corporate training and development, so I've traded in my blackboard for a computer screen! No more chalk on my suits!" She checked the sleeves of her suit to be sure they were chalk free, which, of course, they were.

"I was lucky to get into this field when I did," she continues. "Teaching history at a small southern college, I knew very little about insurance. My Ph.D. wasn't relevant. But teachers were welcome because insurance companies regarded their sales as 'educating' the consumer, teaching them about how insurance helps them manage the risks for themselves and their families."

Starting in the research department, she moved on from there. She became acquainted with many different people in the course of her job, used interviews and questionnaires to gather facts on the industry for internal reports and built a company library.

"I pulled A's at Sweet Briar and always enjoyed being in a classroom, so it made practical sense for me to move to training. Every few years I was promoted. When computers came in, I saw how fearful people were. But this created an opportunity. I asked to learn them myself, so I could teach what I knew to others. My boss was relieved that someone wanted that role, and he sent me to lots of seminars and conferences. It was fun."

She sighed as if the fun was over. "Now that restructuring is again in the wind here, I'm seriously thinking of leaving. I've asked about jobs in other companies, but if you're past forty-five, it isn't easy. Most companies would rather hire somebody younger who'll work for less money.

"So I'm thinking of taking my show on the road—that is, becoming a computer trainer for managers and executives in a variety of companies and industries. I'd like to work for a consulting firm."

She also mentioned a persistent health problem, which meant she didn't dare walk away from her group health coverage.

And if her plan didn't work? "I might like to teach again, but a different topic this time. More relevant to the *real* world."

Beth honed her new career-specific skills in a technical area of training in the insurance industry. That was her core of expertise at the center of her Concentric Career. As she added services for other industries, she built another layer beyond that central core. She could offer free seminars at conferences to attract new clients. She could also market workshops on her own, through universities or associations. These efforts would add another concentric ring to her core. Teaching and writing could add more rings. Lister skills served well in systematic career planning, but they didn't cover all contingencies.

Other examples of Concentric Careers are: academics who teach core sets of courses, and also serve as consultants to industry or government and write books based on this same core expertise; small retail shop owners who start out selling one category, then add items and additional services besides; financial services reps who start with one product, acquire additional licenses and market a wider range of products.

Concentric Careers require the use of Logical and Lister skills to manage the ways the additions relate to each other. You may also pare down your line of offerings as designers do, so that your activities don't undermine each other and so, given market demands, you can focus your energies on what you do best.

Concentric Careers also have built-in safety factors. They don't entail going out very far on a limb. Everything new you add builds on the central core and relates closely to your expertise. As you generate new streams of income, you build additional financial security.

Concurrent Careers

Concurrent Careers are parallel, unrelated careers that you pursue at the same time on more or less parallel tracks. Maybe you love two different occupations and work on both in tandem. You may have transferrable competencies that may serve you well in both arenas, as we'll see in the Competency chapter. Maybe you need two careers to maintain balance in your life. Or, more likely, you have one thing that you do for money and another that you do for love. One career may be in the arts or in some type of social service. Over seven million people hold more than one job—six percent of the total work force. Often they need the extra income to pay bills.

As part of her cure for burnout, Carole became involved with converting city-owned real estate into housing for homeless or poverty-level families. She joined a group of volunteers at her bank working with several nonprofit agencies.

"I want to give something back. I've been lucky, but so many people, especially black men and women, have gone downhill instead of uphill.

Under this program, families who put in 'sweat equity' can end up owning their apartments. They really have to work hard, so the people who benefit really earn what they get. With decent housing, maybe their kids will have more of a chance."

Born on Chicago's South Side, near the university, Carole received her M.B.A. in marketing with a minor in finance from Roosevelt University, while working in banks as an intern. Living with an aunt in the Bronx for a summer, she discovered that she liked the pace of New York and stayed on.

"Of course, not all my motives here are altruistic. This is a marvelous opportunity to learn more about real estate and about building inspection, contractors and all that goes into renovating these buildings, plus the legal red tape. I'm also gaining rapport with people here at the bank who are involved with real-estate investments. They like the perspective I bring to this, the way I keep pointing out alternative outcomes, and I think they'd like me on their team for other projects too.

"You won't believe how this has cured my burnout. After I got really busy with this, I said to myself one day, 'Hey, I like my life and my job and I'm learning something new.' It's just what the doctor ordered!"

Carole was hoping to move into the real-estate division at the bank. This wouldn't happen right away, she realized, but the groundwork had begun. She was willing to devote long hours to her volunteer projects and learning about real estate. This paralleled her marketing job at the bank, giving her Concurrent Careers.

Those who balance Concurrent Careers must have plenty of energy and commitment; they thrive on keeping a lot of balls in the air, learning as they go. Jane Fonda—with her parallel careers as actor, exercise maven and political activist—has three Concurrent Careers. More typically, one career is considerably riskier than the other. Many, like Carole, devote themselves to artistic or activist interests that do not generate income, along with a business or profession that pays the bills. The variety keeps a Learner challenged and flexible. Many times too, both careers are profitable.

How much can you juggle at any one time? To some people more than one career is overwhelming. But perhaps you've already had parallel Concurrent Careers when you were in college and working, or as a mother and homemaker pursuing a career outside your home as well. Having balanced this many responsibilities before, you could surely balance two careers *if* motivated. You might choose to, for example, when entering a new field, keeping your old job for financial security. Or when your job is endangered and you must develop an alternative income source before the ax falls.

"People ask me where I get the energy," said Carole. "When you really care about something, the energy is there. In my case too, I've been recovering from breaking up a relationship, losing my mother and a bad case of job burnout. There were gaps in my life to fill and I found something worthwhile to fill them."

Combination Careers

Combination Careers are a collage or crazy-quilt approach to working—a bit of this, a bit of that. You're able to switch-hit, you crave autonomy and variety. You dread being boxed in at a large organization and being bored by routine. Your diverse pursuits combine in ways that make little sense to other people but fit your own needs and interests.

Diana hoped to leave her cosmetics company for free-lance work, doing writing for publications and speeches for corporate clients as well as for public relations and advertising agencies. At the same time, she wanted to write fiction and a play. It would all be varied and challenging, with some aspects profitable from the start and others with a chance of paying off big or not paying off at all.

"Working at home when my babies were little gave me a sense of the free-lance life. I love it! Sometimes I do my best work while everybody else is sleeping!" Diana said. On weekends she'd been getting up before the rest of the family to work on creative projects.

She first looked at the practical side. She'd published a few articles in magazines and was building her portfolio of writing samples from her on-the-job assignments. "I've tried to get as much experience writing as I can—annual reports, company newsletters, press releases for a lot of different products and audiences. Many writers specialize. I'd like to be able to take advantage of any good opportunity. I've also taken fiction writing courses that improved my descriptive writing and my development of plot and characters."

Diana couldn't predict what projects would surface, but diversity and challenge were more important to her than fitting it all together coherently. She'd do well to cultivate a few bread-and-butter accounts—a newsletter or steady work for hire.

I thought of the importance of people in this Listener's life. "Won't you miss your many colleagues?"

"Oh, I've got to stay connected. I'll come into the city for lunch or to see clients at least once a week. The phone, the fax and electronic mail can't replace sitting down and talking with someone." Her colleagues at work exerted a strong pull on her, but not enough to stand in the way of developing the independent Combination Career she envisioned.

Her Combination Career probably wouldn't show upward progress as in a Classic Career. Some years she might earn more than others. Completing and publishing a novel or writing a play and having it produced were ambitions she dreamed about. Ironically, achieving either of these could mean a cut in income.

However, it was still a dream when we talked. She and Nate needed two steady incomes to support their household of four, and what spare time they had, they spent with their children. One Saturday, she stayed with the kids while he went to a ball game; the next, he stayed while she disappeared to her attic hideaway to work on her stories.

Some people's careers look like patchwork. I'm sometimes at a loss to connect what they've done or to see themes in their work. One woman had a beauty business, sold real estate, modeled and invented a new bra! Another had sold training programs, worked in a prison and next was designing handbags.

Both women exhibited an abundance of energy and ideas. They wanted to do *everything*, though not for long. They were Leapers, as are many with Combination and Contingency Careers. They follow what excites them at the moment and they're motivated by the dream of hitting it big, fast, without necessarily paying their dues.

It's almost impossible to capture some Combination Careers in a résumé. Nothing builds, nothing follows a logical sequence. You have to leave out certain things. One counselor called the process "career patching." There's no way to indicate the potential, the energy, the verve.

Combination Careers are more risky, more problematic, fraught with Domino changes. Many early careers have this look as people skip from job to job before settling on something. Eventually they may clump this hodgepodge into "Other Professional Experience" on their résumés or leave it off entirely.

If you have trouble listing your experiences on a résumé, perhaps you have a Combination Career. If you are energized, earning enough and looking forward to your next project with enthusiasm, fine. But perhaps the promise of excitement keeps you from committing yourself to anything. Commitment itself may seem like closing the door on interesting, though unknown, possibilities.

Sooner or later, you may find yourself between projects for too long, or you may realize that your earnings are far less than if you'd stuck to one thing. Your varied experience doesn't add up to a specific title or credibility that people recognize. You can't point to any particular achievement and you're hard-pressed to demonstrate your potential.

If you're burned out in your Combination Career, you may be ready to transform it into a Concentric Career shape. Look at your core skills and select the strongest, most marketable ones. Start building from there in a more focused, systematic way so that you can enhance your reputation *and* your income. Diana might eventually need to concentrate on one type of writing or one type of client to make free-lancing profitable. Although she could still write fiction and plays, these would be back-burner, spare-time activities, much as they've been in the past, until she could earn enough to risk weeks without income.

Contingency Careers

In retailing, we had contingency squads of skilled salespeople who moved from department to department, as needed. We loved to see them coming because they could usually outsell everybody else. Confident, aggressive, tough, mostly older women who'd been in the store for years, they thrived on the variety and the autonomy. They were paid more and often worked flexible, shorter midday hours.

A Contingency Career, as I define it, is a stopgap measure. It's what you do while you're preparing for the career you really want or waiting for a job or an opportunity to come through. It may not look like a career at all. It may be remote from your core expertise, and it's only temporary.

Contingency Careers are what made Elinor's history as "checkered" as it was. She started at Hunter College with law school in mind, but her grades were only average. Switching to Baruch, also in New York, she majored in retailing, which was much less boring to her. Later she took fashion courses at the Fashion Institute and Parsons, polishing her unique "look" as well as her design and merchandising skills.

Active in student organizations, she used her aggressive energy to speak out on political issues and acquired a reputation as a fighter. I gathered she was pretty obnoxious, full of herself and her opinions in those early years. When I met her, she was still a diamond in the rough, but undeniably, she had potential.

"Retailing was a natural for me, after all those years in my family's pharmacy, then summers at the mall and trendy boutiques during the holiday rush. Must be in my blood." Smoke hung in the air as she lit her third cigarette from the butt of the second.

She squinted her blue mascaraed eyes as she rapidly spewed out her story. "My career has never been a straight-line kind of trip. I jumped from Penney's to Macy's to The Gap during college, trying to find where I fit in. Yeah, I got fired a few times, but it didn't bother me. I could always go somewhere else—even back to the pharmacy—though I really wanted to be independent from my parents.

"Altman's wasn't *me*. I thought Bloomie's would be more my image, but it wasn't a great fit either. I spent a lot of money on the Bloomie's 'look' while I worked there, really a lot, considering how little they paid me. That got to me after a while, how I was supposed to look like our customers, who'd spend what I earned in a week on a dress or a handbag. Don't get me wrong. I love nice things, would love to be able to afford them too. But I'd rather have something ethnic or something I've made than look like a department store display. Know what I mean? When you don't have much money, you'd better be an original." She smiled, confident in the thought that she was one of a kind.

"I finally chose a department store I thought was on the move—in Manhattan. They were changing their image—trendy TV commercials, you know, spiffing up the store. I thought, 'let me grow with them,' as they say."

She held a variety of stopgap jobs between better positions and during a time when she was trying to start a business without backing. Although never returning to a pharmacy, she reverted to selling at boutiques on Columbus Avenue and more recently, tried flea-market selling on the weekends.

"My challenge is to build a solid reputation with my vendors," she said. "I've changed jobs so many times, I don't feel grounded. Every two years it's been something else. It's been great experience, but it would be better for them to see me as a 'star' in my field. I've had some winners." She held up a belt made of fake fur. "But I've also had my share of markdowns. Fortunately my current boss understands that."

Elinor could create excitement, but it didn't always sell. "You have to be a leader, out in front. I'm getting gray hairs from trying." She pointed to her crown but I didn't see any gray. Chic as ever in stark black and white, she paused to frown at her reflection in a dingy mirror tacked to the wall.

"I want my own business. I wouldn't be manufacturing here, of course. I couldn't get the financing for that, at least not legit. Don't even ask about ethics. Aaarrrggghhh . . . My Indian contacts are pretty good, though. I'm good at ferreting out sources of new items. I could do something in imports, maybe mail order. Start small and build cautiously. I'd really have to watch it. I could end up 'eating' a lot of inventory." She seemed to be learning her way around the world of retailing.

My hunch was that when she saw the right opportunity, Elinor would "leap" in, though cautiously, I hoped. Meanwhile, though, she was testing items at flea markets, while earning some loose change on the side, Contingency fashion. At the same time, she was building her core expertise in a Concentric way too. Our Elinor was definitely moving beyond the restrictions of her Leaper style, learning to cope in new ways. She seemed to know what I was thinking. "There's hope for me yet," she said, and I agreed.

Writers and keyboard musicians who do word processing, actors who do telemarketing, artists who do house painting—all are examples of Contingency Careers in which some elementary form of skills and talents is used to earn money to live on. As professionals who skipped the clerical pool or quickly got promoted out of it, we never expected to slide backward to low status and low pay. Today's turbulent employment market, however, demands having contingency plans and perhaps a Contingency Career as well.

It's not easy to hop into a Contingency Career, especially after achieving some status and reputation at something else. When men in business lose their jobs suddenly, they're not likely to take jobs in sales or office work. It's hard to imagine a professional woman like Allison stepping into a lower-echelon job in an emergency. Beth remembered only too well learning typing as she majored in history, "to have something to fall back on," as her Depression-era mother put it. Beth's expertise with computers and computer training assured her of a comfortable stopgap income if she was suddenly out of work.

Women who have more Domino changes can seemingly move into Contingency Careers more easily. Diana could do word processing in a pinch. Carole wasn't so sure. "I've worked too hard to go back to low-paying work. But maybe there's something that pays well that's good experience too. Maybe I could sell real estate or work in property management."

The Learner's attitude toward a Contingency Career is to turn it into a Concurrent Career, or at least a learning experience. Instead of using her expertise at an elementary level, the Learner welcomes an opportunity to acquire new skills or knowledge. If she's never done word processing, she might work where she can learn a popular program. If she has only meager sales skills, she might look for a sales position with on-the-job training. She might also "stretch" into a Contingency arrangement remote from her other career if the pay makes sense—she might paint apartments, trim trees or sell cars—and look at this achievement with pride too.

It can also help to build experience in a Contingency field over time, to prevent having to go back to square one if a crisis hits. Thus, you might produce brochures instead of just proofing them or sell high-ticket items on commission instead of clerking at minimum wage. Contingency employment doesn't have to be a comedown. It can even be fun *if* you've given it some thought and preparation or if you can look at it as a chance to learn and accomplish something new.

No matter what your basic coping style, you can fashion a career in any new shape. You're probably most comfortable in the career shape nearest your coping style on the Change Continuum. As you've surmised, Logicals and Listers lean toward Classic, Concentric and Concurrent Careers, which offer more structure and organization, with changes limited to the more predictable Discrete ones. Contingency and Combination careers have more upheaval and variation, attracting Leapers and Listeners, whose lives have more Domino changes. These career shapes entail more risks, as well as more ambiguity and insecurity, yet allow room for exploring a variety of ways to make money.

Whatever the shape of your career now, you can mold it to meet your changing needs. You might move away from the risk of a Combination Career toward the safety of a Concentric pattern, where you also have variety, yet keep building upon a solid core. Increasingly too, it's wise not to rely solely on one employer. Multiple streams of income provide a hedge against restructuring, downsizing and any of the other things that can and do go wrong.

Each of the five women had plans for change, though in various stages

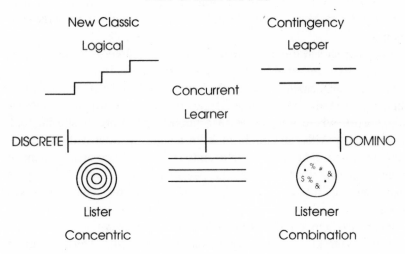

NEW CAREER SHAPES

New Classic · Contingency

Logical · Leaper

Concurrent

Learner

DISCRETE · DOMINO

Lister · Listener

Concentric · Combination

of development. This was true of most of the women I interviewed. Those still working in large companies planned to move on in the next few years. They had worked hard, and in some cases were the highest-level women in their companies. Others who had already made major career moves were successful in ways they'd never have imagined a decade ago.

Career paths today look different over time:

THE CAREER CONTINUUM

1970s—1980s · 1990s—Future

Career Paths Over Time

The single mid-life crisis is represented in the drawing at the left. Career paths now have more zigzags, crises and multiple major changes like the diagram on the right. Roadblocks in your route mean changing course and altering your ambitions. Paths not taken earlier may lead in new directions, while mid-course corrections help fine-tune successful career changes. Skills are transferred to different environments and new skills are added.

The smooth sailing is gone, but we now have many new options for navigating turbulent seas. **What is essential is that you chart a general career direction, and know that you're making progress, achieving goals and getting more of what you want from your work.**

To make sense of your professional future, first look at your past as you did with Your Major Life Changes Exercise. Here's an exercise to help you examine the shapes your career has already had and ones it might take in the future.

EXERCISE I

YOUR CAREER SHAPES

1. Think of each job or career that you've had in the past, referring to your résumé if necessary. Now jot down each past job next to the shape it most resembles.

Career Forms	Past	Present	Future
Old Classic			
New Classic			
Concentric			
Concurrent			
Combination			
Contingency			

Elinor's past included many Contingency periods—when she tried to start a new business while working in sales to make ends meet, when she was unemployed, and early on as a student learning her field in department stores and chains. In each case she had a fallback to support herself while pursuing another goal.

If you're a Leaper you may have similar mixes. If you're a Logical, perhaps your experiences add up to Classic.

2. Now think of your present work. Write it in the Present column on the line for the shape most like it. Do the same for your future. Which shape feels like the best fit for you? Write in what your title might be then.

Whatever your career shape, the choice is yours in designing your future.

YOUR CAREER-SPECIFIC COMPETENCIES

To see how you can build your future on the competencies you already have, look at Beth's Concentric Core of Competencies. She built on her teaching/training abilities. The content of her knowledge about the insurance industry made them career specific, but later we'll see how parts were transferable to other fields too. Note how the competencies relate to each style (Lister, Logical, etc.)

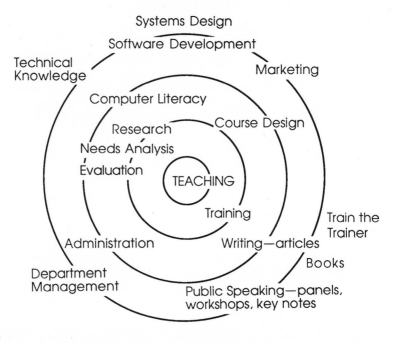

BETH'S CONCENTRIC CORE
OF COMPETENCIES

Of course, Beth could have been much more technical, as she'd have to be in a résumé or interview, but this will give you an idea of how she added to her initial teaching skills over time. The items toward the outer circle were ones she'd like to develop. Now try this yourself.

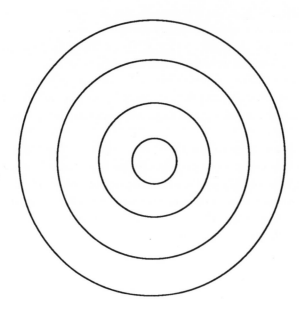

YOUR COMPETENCY CORE

1. Define an area of competency in which you have training and where you can demonstrate your skills on the job. It should be an area that is worth expanding. Fill in as much as you can, as Beth did.

2. This exercise gives you an idea of how to develop your competencies and career in a way that builds on your core. Later you'll see how you can travel with these assets.

PROGRESS REPORT

Our women started out in Classic Careers. With the exception of Allison, all traced new shapes.

Our Lister, Beth, now building a consulting practice on her technical training skills, said, "I'm more comfortable handling a change in an organized way."

Carole was juggling two Concurrent Careers in bank marketing and real estate as her interests shifted and broadened. As a Learner, she liked keeping many balls in the air, making her learning curve steep. "I feel more alive with a new focus for my energies," she said.

Moving toward free-lance writing, Diana had a Combination Career emerging. "I like the autonomy and the variety of clients and projects. Also, I'm sure I have a novel in me and maybe a play too."

"Thank God for Contingency Careers," our Leaper, Elinor, blurted. "They've saved my neck more than once, and probably will again in a pinch."

It's up to you to map out the career path that matches your style and meshes with the other phases of your life. Considering these new career shapes can help you see future possibilities, and new ways you can build on your past experience to reach your future goals. We'll pin down the details later. First we'll look at other phases of your life, beginning with your relationships.

CHAPTER V

Your Roles, Relationships and Balance

CERTAIN relationships can make or break our ambitions. In addition, marriage and often parenthood are ambitions in themselves. Yet our roles and obligations as wives and mothers and as daughters and friends are often in conflict with our professional roles, posing difficult dilemmas and requiring trade-offs that are painful. The balance we want is often hard to achieve.

This chapter will explore women's changing roles over time and how they interact with our ambitions and careers. We'll also look at how our coping styles affect our relationships. The insights you'll gain will help you to shift your relationship/career balance more to your liking and will yield techniques for enhancing all your relationships.

ALLISON'S RELATIONSHIP CHALLENGES

When you first meet a person like Allison—someone who speaks and thinks logically, dresses impeccably and isn't easily perturbed—you might assume that not much has happened in her life. But heart-wrenching things *do* happen to such women. They're just reluctant to talk about them.

In our early interviews, I'd already had hints of the family problems plaguing Allison's ambitions and career. "Come over to the house," she said when I asked for an in-depth discussion on the subject of relationships. Typically, she didn't like discussing anything too personal in her office.

"Where to begin?" she sighed. "Do you want to hear about growing up?"

I told her that would be a good place to start because early influences may still affect our current relationship/career balance.

"My mother worked, but wasn't a career woman. She was in accounts payable and was proud of being able to help out the family. My father worked in operations for the same telecommunications company Keith works for. He never went to college, but he learned a lot about radar technology in the Navy during World War II. And he had a good mind.

"It was Dad who encouraged me to be curious about things. When I was little, he'd take me outside to look at the dew and explain how it happened to be there. Sometimes when Mom was away, he'd turn the kitchen into a chemistry lab. Of course, I loved the attention he gave me, and I enjoyed the intellectual challenge. He taught me to think. None of my teachers in school were as interesting as my Dad. He had a profound effect on my ambitions." And on her Logical style too, I could tell.

"You weren't an only child, though," I prodded.

"No, I have a younger sister, Nadine. I hardly ever see her. She was closer to my mother. In the sixties, she rebelled, ran away from college, and we finally found out she was living with another woman in Santa Fe. And they weren't just roommates." She shook her head. It was clear that Allison didn't understand her sister's choices. She'd made little effort to stay in touch. "Nadine never got along with Dad. And she's not much help now that we have this problem with his Alzheimer's. Well, I suppose she does provide Mom with emotional support by phone and a letter on occasion. . . .

"A couple of years ago, Mom noticed that Dad was becoming vague. First he lost his keys, then he lost the car—walked home from the grocery store without it. I thought Mom was too tough on him, but things got worse very fast. It was diagnosed as Alzheimer's. Of course, we had to keep him from driving, then from walking, because he'd get lost, and it wasn't long before he didn't even recognize me or the kids. We had to find a nursing home for him. . . ."

Although upset, she went on talking in an even voice. "It doesn't make sense to go on living this way. He's a hundred-and-seventy-pound toddler. He's in diapers. He would not have wanted this. He would have taken pills or something if he had realized in time what was happening. The father I knew is gone."

Allison's logical mind was at a loss in coping with something so totally unpredictable and so senseless. She clearly was grieving, just as most people do when someone close has died.

She very capably handled the problems surrounding her father's illness. She investigated nursing homes, helped her mother liquidate certain assets, drew up a budget and, conferring with Keith, set aside a sizable amount they would contribute to her father's care each month. "It's a crunch we hadn't counted on, but what else can you do?" she said.

Allison was sad that her expectations for her parents' happy sunset years were no longer realistic. She lost sleep weeping for her father, worrying about her mother and being angry at her sister. She wasn't accustomed to the depth and complexity of her emotions. Finally she was in a Domino phase, however, and larger questions about the meaning of life were no longer easy for her to dismiss as useless philosophical speculation.

On a few occasions she attended a support group for families of Alzheimer's patients with her mother. "I've never been much for support groups," said Allison, "but Mom wears her emotions on her sleeve and she gets a lot out of it. Sometimes I envy her. Sometimes I wish I could express mine more easily."

This wasn't the only support group she attended in recent years, nor was it her only family problem. Scotty, the once beautiful baby, had become a rebellious teenager.

"We noticed some behavior changes. He'd always been an A student and suddenly he didn't care about school. He started hanging around with kids who were rather unsavory looking. He stopped being polite; he'd have outbursts of temper and was downright rude. We were very concerned. We'd try to punish him by grounding him and he'd sneak out a window. Nothing we tried worked. Then finally, he was arrested for drugs. The police raided a party where everybody was using cocaine. My little boy on cocaine! I'd been so naive!

"As Keith said, 'Now we know what the problem is.' So we looked into treatment programs and got him into one. The people there insisted that Keith and I go to a parent support group.

"In the support group, we've learned that we have to let our kids live their own lives. The stress some parents put on their kids is enormous. We're lucky. Now Scotty is doing better in school and is off drugs."

Allison's father's illness and her son's drug problem took away time and energy she'd hoped to devote to her career. Realizing that she probably couldn't advance further in her company, she would have liked exploring other career options. But these family problems plus her daughter's college expenses meant that she had to match her current high salary. For the moment, her ambitions were on hold.

Men have traditionally been locked into a particular job because of such financial restraints. A man in Allison's position might be discreetly looking for a better-paying job. Juggling her family responsibilities and the demands of her present position was all Allison could manage. "Don't get me wrong. Keith is as helpful as he could possibly be," she added.

Men's careers are generally less affected by what happens in their relationships. Divorce has a great emotional impact on men as well as on women, but it is more likely to change a woman's status adversely. Pregnancy and having children, as well as caring for them, have more impact on women's energy, time constraints and careers too. And when aging parents need care, they tend to look to their daughters.

Far from being problem-free, Allison's life exemplifies many of the problems women confront in their relationships. Let's back up now and look at those relationships and roles one at a time, starting out with our first families, where the seeds of our style and our ambitions were first sown.

FIRST FAMILIES

By first families, I mean families of origin, fathers and mothers and siblings of our childhoods. They help shape our identities and give us our sense of place in the world, as Allison's father did with her. His attitude strengthened her Logical style and motivated her to major in biochemistry, and later to study law as well. She felt unique and secure in her ability to rise to mental challenges. "All my career ambitions spring from him," she said. "My values too." Carole also spoke proudly of her home upbringing, where learning and career ambitions were encouraged.

Not everyone is so fortunate. Beth's story is a struggle to escape abusive, manipulative situations. Her teen years were a fight for control over the chaos of an alcoholic home. "We were always pretending things were fine when they weren't. You know the expression 'Waiting for the other shoe to drop'—that's when I knew I was safe for the night. When Daddy's other shoe dropped when he passed out."

These experiences sharpened her Lister need to bring order to her life. "I learned to keep up appearances," she said. She shared an awesome burden alongside her mother, that of hiding the family problem and projecting an appearance of normalcy. "We did crazy things. Daddy couldn't stand to see us cleaning house, so we'd do it in the middle of the night!" She helped her mother "manage" things in the household, because even the grocery money would have gone for alcohol except for their contriving. "In some ways I was very grown up as a child; in other ways, I'm still not grown up," she admitted. Even at an early age, she broke down Domino events into Discrete elements.

Diana pushed to escape her family for different reasons. "Papa was very strict, very macho." She was raised in California, in the San Gabriel Valley outside Los Angeles, the only girl in a family of five children and the youngest. "My father, who is part Mexican, wanted me to be his little doll.

"I was supposed to live at home until I married, and he'd have married me off pretty young too. He didn't understand that I needed to date different guys or that I wanted an education and a career. My mother would intervene on my behalf." Diana's Listener style is much like her mother's.

"My family expected me to go to one of the state colleges and live at home, but I had a scholarship to Claremont College, a private college inland from Los Angeles, and my art teachers in high school encouraged me to take advantage of the opportunity. I studied art, and did some writing. That was a wonderful time. I still have some of my creations.

"Many of my classmates went on to graduate school. I felt it was time to get involved in the 'real world.' I worked for a West Coast toy company, where I learned to write press releases, among other things. I was learning my trade in that chapter of my life and becoming more independent each year. When my oldest brother moved to New York, I soon followed, got a job with this company and met Nate." Diana's face brightened. Her relationship with her brothers was still "simpatico," she said.

It's not unusual for women to be estranged from siblings, however, as

Allison was from her sister, Nadine. Elinor let years go by without any contact with her brother Paul. Indeed, the residual effects of family problems continue to erode energies, foster angers and undermine a woman's ability to form intimate relationships for years afterward.

A number of my subjects described moving away from their parents' homes as a big step. Elinor's struggle with her family was particularly rebellious, going beyond the typical need to define oneself as an independent person. She felt smothered for years, living with her parents and working with them too, in their pharmacy. "We had clashes. Dad is a perfectionist, very controlling, very hard to please. My brother Paul was just like him. They'd want every label pasted on just so. It drove me crazy. . . ." Virtually any Leaper would have reacted this way.

"My mother drove me crazy in other ways. She'd buy this cheap jewelry for the store, rationalizing that it would sell, then she couldn't part with it! Sometimes there was more jewelry on my mother than on the counter! That's how I developed my taste in accessories." She fingered the lapis lazuli drops that dangled from her ears. "I try to make up for my mother's terrible taste!"

Yet she missed her family more than she'd thought she would when they moved to Florida. They were much easier to get along with in short doses on weekend visits, she discovered. This has improved her relationship with them.

Some women want to be like a strong parent, as Allison wanted to be like her father. Just as often they make a conscious decision to be different from a parent whose style is not theirs or with whom they otherwise clashed. **Our first families influence us in many different ways, and whether we like that influence or not, it's hard to shake it off, even when we're on our own, living very different lives.**

A Family of One

Ten million Americans in their early thirties and under have not yet married. They didn't necessarily plan it this way; a successful single life is rarely if ever a lifelong ambition. More often it's the way things turn out.

In Mary Anne Devanna's study of Columbia M.B.A.'s of 1969 through 1972, only fifty-eight percent of the women had married, versus seventy-three percent of the men. By delaying marriage while establishing careers, these women and others like them say they are running out of "eligible" men. Part of the problem is that women persist in defining "eligible" as older, better educated and with successful careers.

Staying single is more socially acceptable now. Several university studies have found that seventy to eighty-five percent of young women do not believe that being married is better than being single, and are satisfied with their single status. This may change, however, as they draw closer to the end of their childbearing years.

"I've got time," said Elinor at twenty-eight. "Some of my friends are divorced already and they're not even thirty! I see what married men are up to in my field too. They've got too many opportunities to play around. Usually I don't find out they're married until they're ready to move on. Yuck. Such geeks. They want it both ways."

Elinor had had flings with younger and older men, showing little concern for her future. Among her colleagues were older women involved with younger men. These women had a Leaper's flair for excitement too. Elinor assumed she'd always be able to attract somebody who turned her on.

Carole had been ready to settle down when she met Malcolm, who actually had many of the characteristics of a good husband. "He was a homebody, hardworking, loved to talk—he'll make somebody a very nice mate!" After the breakup, she was reluctant to start dating. Her sister, Roanda, now a model in Paris, told Carole the prospects were better abroad. "Maybe I should transfer overseas," she said, ever the Learner, seeking new challenges. She wasn't looking for excitement, though. She wanted commitment from a man. "I'll add the spice!"

Among the women in my research, a number had been divorced in their late twenties or early thirties. Most had a sense of failure, in spite of having ex-husbands who were gay, alcoholic, abusive, too competitive or too passive. It took them several years to recover. Meanwhile they concealed their pain at work and threw themselves headlong into careers. Only one out of eight divorcées in my sample has remarried. Nationally, fewer divorced women remarry than do men.

However, professional women do not marry simply for the sake of being married or to enhance their chances for career success. Their reasons are far more personal: They want intimacy and companionship. Some women have gone to a lot of trouble trying to find suitable men. They've tried singles events, classified ads, video dating and match-makers as well as charity, religious and political groups. Almost nothing works. A few women are dating younger men or those with less income or professional achievement; their more realistic expectations allow men to be human too. Women with children have an even harder time. Yet people somehow do manage to combine his, hers and theirs in new kinds of families!

Beth laughed at the folly of her early dreams. "My idea of heaven was to marry a Southern scholar, settle down in a big house with a veranda, raise four or five kids and then maybe volunteer for the hospital.

"Well, I got the scholar for a husband but the rest of the fantasy didn't come together." Beth almost gave up on dating until meeting Lawry when she was in her forties. "My first marriage was such a blow to my self-esteem I wouldn't go near anyone who'd have more than one drink. Friends tried to fix me up, but so many of those guys were interested only in themselves or I just didn't have anything in common with them. I'd just as soon stay home with a good book!"

Large numbers of women feel this way; they're not putting their lives on hold. They're buying homes and condos, making serious investments, traveling, not letting their single status slow them down. These single women often select houses or apartments with room for entertaining their family-like constellations of friends. They may stage annual parties as traditions of their own to share with friends and extended family. One woman holds an annual potluck networking party for women only. Beth entertained her women friends often, and included her boyfriend's daughter, Pam, in these gatherings.

Even after carving out an exemplary life for themselves, women don't abandon hope of finding a partner. "I certainly don't plan to spend my life alone," said Carole, who tries to ignore the statistics for black women her age—only thirty percent are living with a husband, down from seventy percent in the 1950s. She began making investments and creating a full life, yet she hoped to be one of the exceptions. Where marriage is concerned, so many women hope to beat the odds. Trying to tip the odds in their favor, they turn down transfers to small towns and foreign countries where eligible men may be scarce. Some women share their living space with partners who may or may not make long-term commitments.

LIVING WITH SOMEONE

Other women have roommates, often female, and more commonly now, platonic male friends. Elinor, having had both types of roommates, much preferred having her own place. Besides the privacy, she liked having the option of sharing it if she met someone exciting.

Over 2.6 million U.S. households are couples living together. It used to be called "trial marriage," but many such couples don't discuss marriage. Living together can be an alternative to commitment. In *The Couple's Journey*, Susan Campbell describes the stages couples pass through from romance to power struggle to stability to commitment and creating a life together. Often couples get stuck at the power struggle or commitment stage, fearing the next step. They're struggling over who pays for what, equality, equity, who loves whom most. Sometimes both partners go to encounter or couples' workshops or to therapy to work things out.

Women frequently complain about men's reluctance to commit themselves. A woman who is eager for marriage and determined not to waste time may issue an ultimatum, giving her lover the choice of marriage or breaking up.

But it is increasingly the woman who is gun-shy, as Beth was. Even after these many years, remarriage wasn't a priority for her. In her first years in New York, she led a quiet social life centering around work, her church and volunteering at a foundling home. The people she met became her new "family." In the early eighties she invested in a two-bedroom apartment when her building went co-op. A small inheritance from her grandmother made up most of the down payment. Lawry, the man in her life, moved in and helped with the monthly payments and expenses.

"Lawry entered my life six years ago," said Beth. Lawrence O'Brian, fifty-seven, was a widower. "Slowly and carefully, we've built a relationship. We advise each other like mentors and partners. We've talked of being partners in a consulting business. He could open lots of doors for me. I could spark his ambitions."

Although a Logical, Lawry was undergoing a series of Domino events during their first years together. Beth was extremely helpful. "He'd been a partner for seventeen years at a major international accounting firm. They told him he'd have to market more and bring in new business, but he never thought they'd fire him. He'd had a mild heart attack and was recovering nicely when the creeps let him go. I couldn't believe it," Beth explained.

"He felt betrayed. It was terrible. They kept him on salary for six months and gave him outplacement help, but it's not easy finding a new job at his age with a heart problem. It took all of my energy to support him emotionally, but it drew us closer together. We're committed now, but not ready to tie the knot just yet. Maybe by the next time we talk."

Lawry probably would do well to grab such a generous partner. Beth was the holdout. She feared another failure, and although Lawry wasn't an alcoholic or an abusive person, she saw parallels with her past. "He isn't the problem. I am. I'm a 'rescuer,' as I learned long ago in twelve-step programs. When Lawry became ill, I was in my element, trying to make it all better." Like Allison, Beth had to learn that there were things she couldn't control. She was working with a therapist to gain insights into her attitudes and behavior and improve her relationship with Lawry and Pam.

Besides emotional closeness, living under the same roof has practical advantages. With living costs at unprecedented highs, pooling resources enables couples to live better. Living together is socially acceptable now in circles that condemned it not long ago. In the 1980s Beth had no need to hide Lawry from her church friends. Yet such couples lack the legal protection of married couples. When Lawry had his heart attack, Beth needed special permission to visit him in the hospital. However, he provided for her in his will so that she wouldn't lose the co-op. Many people jeopardize their future security by not taking such steps.

Homosexual couples face these same issues, plus those faced by minorities. They may also decline to discuss their liaisons with co-workers, revealing their private lives only to the most trusted friends. Telling family members may be a problem too, as Allison's sister Nadine found. Yet many make strong commitments to partners, even holding ceremonies with friends to celebrate their joint venture in life. Many are also campaigning for legal recognition of their relationships, recognition that would benefit heterosexual couples living together as well.

MARRIAGE

A total of ninety-five percent of all those over forty-five "make it official" by marrying at least once. Younger men in their thirties particularly are pressured to do so, because married men are often regarded by employers as more stable and therefore better workers. Some women acknowledge that being married is a career asset for them too. They may entertain bosses or clients after hours with spouses along. A husband is an advantage in fields such as sales where spouses are often involved.

Diana and Nate lived together first. "We have such different backgrounds I wasn't sure it would work. We had family problems to overcome. My Jewish in-laws had grave doubts about me. But Nate hadn't felt so alive in years. I loved the way he romanced me—flowers, candy, champagne for two, little notes on my pillow. And long talks till real late. We couldn't get enough of each other. It's been eight years and I'm still on my honeymoon!" She flushed a bit at the thought.

Her Listener skills were an asset in her marriage. "We never take each other for granted. We share everything and talk our problems out. We don't argue so much as listen to the other's point of view. We're both flexible and easy with each other, even more so since I was ill and we saw how fragile life can be."

Keith and Allison were more of a classic couple. They're both Logicals with families who'd known each other for years. They started dating when she was a sophomore and he was a senior in college. "Keith and I were college sweethearts in Boston when he was at Northeastern in engineering and I was at Boston University. We seemed to think alike. We enjoyed skiing and camping, being off on our own exploring nature. He was more of a friend at first. We grew on each other. We didn't live together. He graduated from college and had to put in his time in the army while I finished. We got married as soon as I got my degree."

After Keith's stint in the service, he joined a large telecommunications company and they bought the house in Teaneck, where they've lived ever since, except for the two years in Houston.

"Now I can't imagine not being together. We're best friends. He advises me on technical things like computers, about office politics and how men are likely to think. I advise him on his rights, on legal policies and how working women think. Way back when, we had up-front discussions about splitting the household load. We've shared everything, even dirty diapers!"

Keith at forty-eight was a tall, graying beanpole of a man, with a shy grin and a twinkle in his blue eyes. The two had their own language and signals, often finishing each other's thoughts. They don't argue. "We debate!" Allison declared.

Married women I interviewed often referred to the emotional as well as financial support their husbands provided. Looking back on facing discrimination, starting a business or dealing with corporate politics, they often said, "I couldn't have made it without him!" When a husband says, "I couldn't have made it without *her*," he means his wife has been his sole source of emotional support, as Daniel Levinson found. Men have traditionally had their wives' support in achieving their goals. Single women, on the other hand, miss out on the help that many of the forty-seven million people who are now part of dual-career marriages can give to each other—financially and in other ways too. Professional couples can strategize about work, balance their careers for the benefit of the whole family, and build a life as partners on a team, if they choose.

Yet it's often a delicate balance of egos and assets. Husbands may feel threatened by their wives' success or independence especially when such changes come suddenly. The husbands of reentry women or women who make a late commitment to their careers often have difficulty adjusting to a deal that's not what they bargained for.

Five million working wives now earn more than their husbands. When one spouse has more of something—money, ambition, brains, beauty, experience or "breeding"—a couple must make trade-offs and compromises in the spirit of doing what's best for both.

Spouses often have trouble telling their mates what really hurts and what they really want. If one partner is jealous or competitive or refuses to help out, the feelings on both sides need to be aired. Of the women I interviewed, several identified unconscious sabotage as a reason their marriages had failed.

Men and women *still* have different views of marriage, according to research from three universities. Men want someone with looks, women want someone with earning power. He wants her to make love and share interests. She's concerned about how he treats her parents and friends, and whether he'll be faithful. Men believe they're doing better in the ways women want; women say they're not. Let's face it. We *want* men to change—our husbands, our boyfriends, our sons, our bosses, and our fathers.

Men have it tougher these days. Behavior that used to be considered normal for them now gets flak. A man doesn't get to sit with his feet up reading the paper and sipping a cocktail while his wife rustles up supper and keeps the kids out of his way. Supper and kids are his responsibility too. If they're partners in breadwinning, most women feel, men must also be partners in other phases of keeping the household together.

Slowly they're getting it. If we ask them to try on our shoes, they empathize to an extent. If we thoughtfully tell them what we expect of them, they know we mean business. Increasingly, women have decided that they will forge ahead in their careers and men will have to understand. Men who don't may not be right for us anyway. That was Elinor's attitude. Carole's too. These women had no intention of jeopardizing their professional lives to accommodate a relationship—not yet anyway.

Classic couples like Allison and Keith will prevail, yet there's an ever-widening variety of new models for intimate relationships. One husband and wife, married eight years, live in separate apartments a few blocks from each other and spend three nights a week together. Another is "bi-coastal," which is becoming increasingly common. They've lived on opposite coasts for twelve years, have two kids and a twenty-five-year marriage. A divorced couple shares a home, each occupying a wing, with the kids in the middle. They have separate bathrooms, separate bedrooms and definitely separate closets. Woody Allen and Mia Farrow have two apartments, nine children whose nurturing they share, and careers that have become symbiotic.

Tradition isn't the limiting factor anymore. Couples are restricted only by their own imaginations, flexibility and, of course, economic resources. Marriage in the years ahead *can* be more of a partnership between equals, both of whom work, both of whom have changing ambitions. Roles can blend and overlap.

Among couples who are more traditional in their outlook, the threat to male egos when wives work is decreasing. More likely, a husband has a new sense of pride in his wife's achievements. In the best of situations, each spouse is lover, mentor, adviser, sounding board and best friend to the other. Each wants to see the other maximize his or her potential, and for each, a compatible relationship is an ambition worth working toward.

BECOMING A PARENT

A major question for the professional woman is: Will I or won't I? Over sixty-five percent of high-level professional women have not had children. Some undoubtedly *chose* not to have families. Others delayed having children until their careers were well launched and their negotiating positions for parental leave were stronger. It is estimated that only fifteen percent of Baby Boom women will remain childless. Just a generation ago, women planned their working lives around their children. Women today are more likely to plan their children, if they have them, around their careers. Indeed, there is a Baby Boomlet created by Baby Boomers, some having babies in their forties.

David Bloom of Harvard reports that professional women who delay childbirth past age twenty-seven earn ten percent more, and those without children earn fifteen to twenty percent more than those who have children earlier. Yet seventy percent of U.S. babies are born to women in their twenties. With career fields changing so rapidly, no one can afford to stay away long. In fact, sixty-five percent of new mothers who take maternity leave return within a year.

At Catalyst we saw many high-achieving women who were also mothers. Many had live-in help, sometimes a whole household staff, while they gave long hours to their careers. But few families can afford such assistance.

Increasingly, child care is a recruiting issue and not just a women's issue. Some companies now offer child-care credits, data banks of resources and working parents' groups. At a Minneapolis company sixty percent of young men felt family concerns were affecting their ambitions, reported the *Wall Street Journal.* Surely companies and lawmakers will eventually conclude that it's in everybody's best interest to help families with small children and to retain highly trained women on some basis.

Currently sixty percent of mothers of children under six are in the work force, two thirds of pregnant women work into their last trimester and two thirds of them return to work within three months after their babies are born. Women obviously have a strong commitment to working outside their homes, and for most, leaving their jobs is simply not an option.

Parenthood itself has changed too. More single professional women are becoming single parents, couples unable to bear children have more adoptive strategies to try and unwed fathers are speaking up about their rights. Being a parent is more complex in ways our own parents and Dr. Spock never imagined.

Professional couples wrestle with such dilemmas as whose career goes on hold, who'll stay home if a child is sick (one survey said ninety-seven percent of the time the woman does), how to handle overtime, travel (thirty-eight percent of traveling workers are women) and whether or not to relocate. Each family is charting new ground.

Beth didn't hear the ticking of her biological clock as loudly as some women because arthritis struck when she was just thirty-four, zapping her energy and making her own survival the top priority. Although she had no children of her own, she became "mother" to many in her profession. Also, like many women today, she developed a special relationship with her boyfriend's offspring, in this case Lawry's daughter, Pam, who was nineteen when they met.

Diana hadn't expected motherhood to be so complicated. Shushing her two so we could talk, she looked at the bike jackknifed by the sofa and the decapitated doll in the corner. "When my brothers and I were growing up in California, we were outside all the time. We sort of took care of each other. Mama was home to soothe us if we ran into trouble. I'm sure she worried, but we were healthy, survived lots of childhood accidents and turned out okay.

"It's so different with my kids. With me working, we juggle child care and four schedules. Nate pitches in a lot. My father rarely did. He worked long hours, and there were certain things he thought men shouldn't do. He'd cook, but he'd never clean up. He also cheated. I think Mom knew. . . ."

Her Jason, now seven and slightly dyslexic, needed special classes and follow-up at home, which took more money and time as well. Kimmy, a feisty little redhead, was somewhat hyperactive and by Diana's definition, "a handful," requiring more attention and more supervision. "We don't want her on medication," Diana explained. "My two are more trouble than Mama's five. But I wouldn't trade them, not for anything. Each has different needs, different qualities. We'll try to help them become the best they can be without pressuring them." Their difficulties were a challenge to her, and were what made them unique. Kimmy now dozed as we talked, but her voice intruded on many of our taped conversations.

After the birth of her son, Allison worked part-time and had the benefit of a live-in care giver, Mattie. Six years later, Mattie left to nurse her own mother in the South. "That's when the juggling really started," Allison said wryly. "Between au pairs who might stay for a year, those who didn't work out and some child-care arrangements here in Teaneck, I think we've tried them all. As much as I'd like to plan everything in advance, it just doesn't always work."

Raising teenagers presents its own set of problems, as Allison learned. "I thought I'd have a normal work schedule once Scott was in his teens, but his drug problem took a lot of time and attention. Things are better now." The parent-support group she and Keith attended appealed to Allison's need to take definite actions and expect definite results. They needed to follow up on their son's activities and be sure he kept his end of the bargain, which took time. Yet, where youngsters are concerned, the ultimate results can't always be anticipated. Allison was finally letting go of the dream she once had for her son. "He won't have the Ivy League education and all the advantages that go with it. That was my vision and Keith's, but not Scotty's. We have to step back and let him be his own person."

Allison explained what she learned in her support group: "A legitimate ambition for a parent is to be a good parent. Becoming the mother of a doctor is not a legitimate ambition. It's a dream, but it could be a very unrealistic one." Allison may yet be the mother of a doctor; her daughter Kathy was taking pre-med courses and doing well in them.

Even youngsters who don't get into trouble may develop ambitions far different from their parents' expectations. Young people from middle-class families often major in subjects unrelated to careers. They may opt for blue-collar jobs or join cults or become romantically involved with individuals their families detest. Parents are often disappointed by grown youngsters not taking the paths they'd hoped.

Sometimes those paths lead back to the nest we thought had emptied. A startling proportion of young adults is still living at home. Reasons may have to do with high rents, early divorces, careers that didn't work out, and in some instances, reluctance to grow up. Parents coping with "boomerang" kids need to learn the same lessons Allison learned—let go of unrealistic dreams for them, set firm rules in the home and demand adult behavior. Support groups are helpful here too.

BECOMING PARENTS TO OUR PARENTS

Allison had plenty of company as her friends and contemporaries were catapulted into the "sandwich" generation, caught between the needs of their children and their own parents. Becoming a parent to one's own parents, however, is an often abrupt role reversal that most of us aren't prepared for emotionally or financially. One out of every four over-forty workers, seventy-five percent of them women, are caring for aging parents in some way. The problem will only get worse with the "graying" of our population.

Beth's widowed mother, stricken with one ailment after another, had apparently given up. Beth couldn't persuade her to venture out of her home. "I hoped she would travel. She really deserves a break," said Beth.

Some women are caring for parents, or in some instances, in-laws, aunts or uncles, in their own homes. They've barely emptied the nest when it's filled again. Some care for ailing family members while continuing to do paid work, and some have been forced to give up their jobs to provide almost round-the-clock care. Even if the patient is grateful and courteous, the situation is difficult. Often, though, the patient is far from content. Wills may clash harshly or unresolved family tensions may surface. The stress can be almost immeasurable. Such care givers sometimes collapse from exhaustion.

Some corporations now provide counseling to employees with ailing parents and refer individuals to consultants who help find solutions. The American Association of Retired Persons is one of several resources to provide information on financial options and a list of consultants.

While parenting our parents shifts our role and view of ourselves, it is death in first families that often triggers a major reevaluation of who we are and why we're doing what we do. One woman was still dealing with the deaths of a sister and mother seven years later. In my research, I heard women speak of their mothers' deaths, which might have been decades ago, as if it were yesterday. When a parent dies prematurely, you're struck by the unfairness, as Carole was. If you are middle-aged when a parent dies, you may simultaneously confront your own mortality.

Carole's parents both died before she reached mid-life. "I'd lost my father five years before, but Mama was the family's center, its anchor. I felt like I was in quicksand . . . without foundations anymore. Suddenly _I_ was the grownup, taking care of my sisters. I'd never felt so abandoned, so betrayed, so angry in a way. She wasn't supposed to go yet. I hope _I_ can be as strong as she was someday." Having survived the thing she dreaded most, Carole became stronger.

The pain never totally disappears, but as it subsides, which takes months or maybe a year or two, most of us emerge with more self-reliance and, very likely, a greater awareness of reality and of our own priorities. Our ambitions are more grounded in the realm of possibilities. We may also have a sense of time running out, a new urgency to realize our ambitions.

EXTENDED FAMILY AND FRIENDS

Women I interviewed spoke of reunions with high school friends, college sorority sisters, friends from past places of work. These were links to the past, people who knew "my whole story," as one woman put it. Friends from our adolescence, teen and college years knew us when our future ambitions were amorphous, fragile things. They remember how we tested our abilities, when we stumbled, and, perhaps too, how determined we were.

Women's friendships need little to sustain them over the years. Once the relationship is established, a special connection stays intact. During times when face-to-face meetings are impossible, an occasional phone call will suffice. Diana's friends included men as well as women, people of all ages, in fact. She followed up on long-term friendships better than most, sending notes and photos to her many old friends on the West Coast.

In some friendships whole years go by with only holiday cards and a note, perhaps not even that. Yet the intimacy, the caring and the ability to relate are restored almost instantly. How comfortable these friendships are, compared to the anxiety we experience when a lover is a few hours late in calling!

Some women make a point of keeping in contact with old friends over the years. Beth was one who did. She chose her friends carefully, taking years to build trust. She'd cherished certain relationships for a lifetime and always remembered birthdays, anniversaries and special events. Her gifts were practical things like soap or warm mittens. She was conscious of friends' time constraints too, shooing them out the door on work nights. At her twenty-fifth reunion at Sweet Briar, Beth felt "at home," she said. "These women knew me when." Others note that at reunions women easily take up where they left off, finding common areas of interest even if their lives have taken quite divergent paths.

A recent Smith College twenty-fifth-year reunion held a special panel, where one woman after another, many distinguished in their fields, spoke about missing her friends. Each had concentrated so intently on her own career and family that she'd lost track of many friends. The reunion reminded them how important these friends were. It's unfortunate that maintaining friendships is rarely among the future goals we list for ourselves early in our lives. We learn to appreciate friends more as time passes.

Letty Cottin Pogrebin's *Among Friends* describes at length the role of friends in our lives, how we select them and what we do with them. The women in my research, who spoke mainly of friends as sources of support during major changes, also spoke about the death of a friend as one of life's major events.

For many professional women—whether single, divorced, married with or without children—friends are like members of an extended family. Elinor, in her more volatile manner, said what she felt to many of her friends, sometimes without thinking. She was often angry with her friends, and she made them angry with her. Yet she creatively enticed them back with a clever apology, a gift or a gimmick. She forgave easily and expected the same of others.

Whether working in urban centers with a large circle of friends and acquaintances or in small towns in rural areas, women develop and nurture these friendships each in her own way. For friendships form the backdrop against which our ambitions are crystallized, pursued and realized.

BOSSES AND COLLEAGUES

The workplace can be first family redux for some people. Individuals recreate their families and take up old roles, as Harry Levinson explains with his view of CEOs as fathers and companies as family systems.

Many men don't question hierarchical structures and feel comfortable once they know their place. Some women, especially Leapers like Elinor, resist authority figures. "When my boss tells me to do something, I start figuring out how I can avoid doing it. Or I think to myself, 'I don't have to listen to this. I know what to do,' " Elinor confessed. Listening to the boss is usually in one's own best interests, but Elinor kept playing out the rebellious child fighting her parents. It took therapy and a few firings before Elinor saw how she created problems for herself.

Others compete with the boss. So you're smarter, better educated, more sophisticated, have better family connections. Flaunt it, though, and you're torpedoed. Some very bright women have sabotaged their own careers this way—again and again! "They were such incompetents, I couldn't help it," said one. She could have and should have downplayed the differences *if* her own career progress mattered.

Still others see peers as sibling rivals. They suspect back-stabbing or competitive moves even when none exist. They're jealous when the boss gives the slightest attention to someone else or when anyone else gets recognition.

Then there are bosses who treat employees of all ages as daughters and sons. They mete out punishment, deliberately ignore them and play favorites in a misuse of power that keeps anxiety at peak levels. Punishing bosses have crews of "walking wounded" who haven't escaped, but have taken untold abuse for reasons hard to imagine.

These strange games are also played in academia, government agencies, everywhere people work. Professional associations aren't exempt either, especially in times of industry scandals or cutbacks. Frightened people may revert to insecure behaviors and end up sabotaging others, instead of pulling together to improve the situation.

When you find yourself in the middle of a group of adults behaving absurdly, try to see the behavior in terms of family dynamics. Your insights about why they're doing these things can yield strategies for better coping and maintaining your self-esteem while figuring out what to do next. You'll see that it's not really *you* that your boss or rival is belittling. You'll also see that a powerless father figure protecting his turf may have set up a no-win situation among his subordinates. Things may not get better as long as he's there.

Beth once made a startling discovery. "My boss was sleeping with my secretary. I felt like I was in a soap opera!" Carole had a boss who was jealous of her, tried to undermine her confidence and bad-mouthed her behind her back at every opportunity. "That's life in the trenches," she said.

Analyzing relationships was once considered the province of women. Increasingly, though, men see the value of such insights and businesses make use of them too. Some companies now order psychological assessments of executives before key promotions, lest old "baggage" interfere with success in the new role. Employee assistance and outplacement counseling also provide support in dealing with complex workplace relationships.

OUR STYLE AND RELATIONSHIPS

Your coping style, of course, has a powerful effect on your relationships. Allison was perhaps fortunate that her husband Keith was also a Logical, but their son was a Leaper and their daughter, a Listener. Allison wished they'd be more rational and know why they reached their conclusions. To please someone like Allison, try communicating in a more logical, organized way. Be prepared to back up your intuitive ideas with sound arguments.

Beth's first husband drove her crazy with his Leaper messes, but he felt the same way about her Lister neatness, order and endless details. While he was hosting a party and encouraging everybody to have another drink, she was emptying the ashtrays. Many couples have similar conflicts. One is more emotional, messier and more often late, while the other is tidy about everything and arrives at the party before the hostess has her dress on. Such a pair can get along, however, if each is aware of the differences, seeing them as complementary strengths.

If you have a Lister in your life whom you'd really like to please, be a little more neat. At home, clean up that makeup mess, get your clothes on hangers or into the hamper, wipe up the hairs in the sink. At the office, keep your papers in piles or, better yet, try to overcome your fear of filing. Remember this person values results. Try to understand his or her need to banish chaos and don't add to it. Then try to use that person's abilities synergistically with your own.

To get along with Listeners like Diana, communicate with feeling and stories. Meet them face to face, rather than through memos. Mirror their body language subtly. Don't be judgmental or critical, but give them feedback so they'll know how they're doing. Let them nurture you with their support, which can help you heal. Try to return the support too. They'll let you know when they need it.

If your boss or friend is a Leaper, being too rigid or inflexible is a sin in their eyes. Strive to get on their wavelength: Be enthusiastic about their ideas and creations. Expect them to get mad sometimes and know that they'll expect your forgiveness. They may appreciate your being more organized or analytical if they're smart about their weaknesses. They can be fun and beguiling, but also exasperating. They do make life interesting.

With Learners there's less need to match styles. Avoid routine with them; surprise them with startling discoveries, insights and challenges. Help them grow, even if they're the boss, and learn along with them!

Being aware of these differences can help you form valuable alliances at work. Not only that, you can be more in tune with individuals close to you—spouses, parents, kids and friends—whose behavior and demands are baffling sometimes. The more effectively you cope with all these important relationships, the better odds you have of getting the things you really want both in your career and with the people you love.

Key roles and relationships alter ambitions in ways you might not predict. Families, lovers, marriage partners, children and friends all

add to the complexity of your own unique relationship constellation. There'll be different mixes in the future as your life changes in relation to other people's. In the following exercises, we'll look at what those changes might be, how to manage them and prepare for the outcomes you want.

YOUR RELATIONSHIPS CONSTELLATION

To see how her current relationships support her (or not), Carole placed herself in the center of the concentric circles below. Next, using a colored pencil or pen, she placed her closest supporters around her in the second circle from the center. Moving outward, she wrote the names of the friends and associates who are part of her network. Those less close to her are further from the center. This shows she had no close relationships with men.

CAROLE'S CONSTELLATION

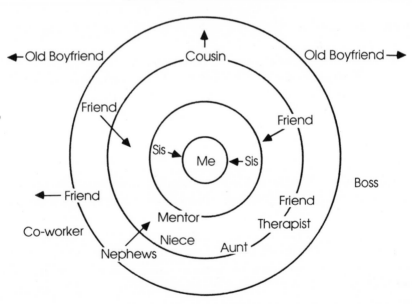

Your Relationships Constellation

1. Place yourself at the center of the concentric circles below as Carole did. Place your closest supporters around you in the second ring. Moving outward, write the names of the friends and associates who are part of your network. Place those who are less close to you further from the center.

2. Next, analyze which friends you'd like to move closer, which further away with arrows pointing in the direction you plan to move them, as Carole has done. This way you can assess your current support system and see what needs to be changed, what's missing.

3. Look at *your* gender, age, support and expertise mix. Does your constellation include a mix of all the styles—Logicals, Listers, Learners, Listeners and Leapers? What changes would *you* like to make? _____

_____

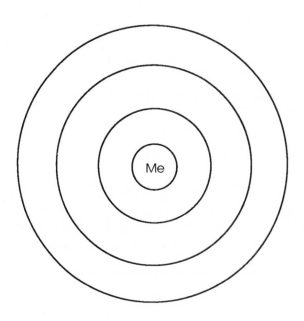

YOUR RELATIONSHIPS AND ALTERED AMBITIONS

Think about each of your relationships listed below and note which have altered your ambitions in the past or might in the future.

Relationship	Past Influence	Future Influence
Mother		
Father		
Siblings		
Teachers		
Mentors/Bosses		
Therapists		
Friends		
Lovers/Spouses		
Children		
Role Models		
Others		

Are you surprised at any of these influences on your ambitions? You may have affected others in a similar manner, or may yet do so. **Recognizing the influences can help you decide to manage them differently from now on.** The next exercise will help you solve problem areas one at a time.

YOUR CONFLICT RESOLUTION

As you completed the first two exercises in this chapter, you may have found some conflicts or relationships you'd like to alter. Here's an exercise to help you. You'll need three or four sheets of paper and colored pens or crayons.

1. On a separate piece of paper, draw a symbol for yourself and another for someone with whom you are in conflict. (One person might be represented by a heart, another by a dollar sign.) Don't worry if it's not great art. It's the *process* of drawing that's the helpful part.

2. Now draw these symbols closer together on a second sheet of paper. It's okay if they change shape.

3. Next draw the symbols intertwined or relating to each other. They might overlap or share a common boundary. Continue to make drawings until you feel less conflict about the relationship or see it in a different, more harmonious way. How have things changed? How might you act differently to resolve the conflict? Perhaps you need to add a third symbol if the conflict involves a triangle of relations. Discuss it with someone you think may provide additional insights.

Use this exercise also to help resolve family versus career, baby versus income, or other dilemmas you may be facing. The purpose is to move you off dead center so you can see new possibilities. Making the drawings taps a different, nonverbal area of your brain, which gives you a new slant on a familiar issue. If the problem is one of style, appreciating someone else's strengths and understanding how he or she operates can help you in approaching that person.

PROGRESS REPORT

The five women learned a lot from the exercises. Allison saw how few work colleagues were in her constellation, also how far away her sister had become. "I guess I have less in common with people at work these days. But I'd better deal with my sister. I'm not looking forward to the Conflict Resolution Exercise, but I'll give it a shot. Maybe tomorrow."

Beth realized several things. "I wasn't sure where to put Lawry. I'd position him real close, move him out a little. I'm battling ambivalence there. I also noticed that I have very few young people in my life. Maybe I should volunteer to work with teenagers."

Carole conceded, "Okay, this demonstrated what I'd suspected. It's time I had a real strategy for meeting men. Maybe I should travel. I'll call Roanda in Paris and let her know I'm on my way!"

"I don't need any more people in my life," Diana laughed. The chapter had brought home to Diana how many people she was nurturing. Her constellation ran off the page. She drew a face to represent each person and called it her mandala.

Elinor's constellation was a rainbow of colors, going from red hot in the center to cooler blues and greens on the edges for her cooler relations. "I really need an anchor relationship," she decided. "I'd like someone older who could help me focus, back my business, be a partner *and* a lover. I'd give him zest for life, a new energy and aliveness. That's a fair trade, don't you think?" She gave me a conspirator's wink.

As you can see, relationships intertwine with all women's ambitions. Next, we'll look at how health issues can add further complications to your career, relations and ambitions.

CHAPTER VI

Your Ambitions and Your Health

No one is ever prepared for the betrayal of the body. We wonder, *How can this be? Why me? Why now?* Maybe recovery is in store, but even so, we've lost a certain innocence about the nature of things. We know for sure if we didn't already that life isn't fair. **Our health can skew our ambitions as nothing else can, not even relationships and role changes or career upheavals.**

A recent survey asked women what they feared most. Number one for those over thirty was the fear of becoming seriously ill. The emotional and professional and career sacrifices can be staggering, as you'll see. But you'll see too that there are ways to survive with the worst illness, design a more healthful life-style and work around the body's betrayal. **The better you understand how your coping style, your ambitions and your health relate, the better you'll be able to cope with whatever the future may hold.**

We've already witnessed Diana's cancer scare, her panic response and her coming to terms with her mortality. The fact that we are mortal is perhaps the most important lesson of all in understanding the context in which we can realize our ambitions. Life is, after all, a race with time. None of us has time for all the things we'd like, so we're forced to make choices.

Other types of health problems hold important lessons for us as well. A degenerative disease such as arthritis is hardly a crisis. It may strike suddenly, but its ravages are slow and continuing. Many people don't have to confront such diseases until late in their careers and their lives when they've reached many of their goals. Beth wasn't so lucky.

BETH MEETS THE CHALLENGE OF ARTHRITIS

Beth had adjusted nicely to living in New York by the time she was thirty-four. "Things at work were stressful, however. This was when I'd discovered that my boss was sleeping with my secretary. They'd be gone for hours together, leaving me to hold down the fort, and I'd wonder what they were saying about me or what they might be plotting.

"One Saturday I was working at home. I used yellow legal pads in those days, and I'd brought home a supply of freshly sharpened pencils. After I'd worked for an hour or so, my right hand began to hurt. I found a softer pencil so I wouldn't have to press so hard, but it kept hurting and my knuckles began swelling later that day too."

The pain did not go away. The next week she saw her internist, a woman. "I knew she wouldn't dismiss what I felt as not being important. She asked if anyone in my family had arthritis. I had to tell her yes, but I still didn't think it could be happening to me. Those great aunts with arthritis were so old. Later tests confirmed the diagnosis."

Beth switched to another department in the insurance company. She was grateful to be working with different people, but her problem only became worse. "The other hand became swollen and my whole body became stiff in the mornings. My ankles, then my knees and hips were under siege by the time I was thirty-seven." As she spoke, I noticed her shifting her position in her chair and rubbing her hands.

Aspirin helped a little, but not much. She tried every drug on the market. "I'd get my hopes up when something seemed to work, but nothing has ever worked for very long." She also tried copper bracelets, guided imagery, exercise, special diets, all without lasting relief. What has helped are hot baths, extra Excedrin and when it's *really* bad, codeine.

By the age of forty, she was working in her company's training department and traveling a lot. "I developed the habit of always looking for an opportunity to sit down. Thank heaven for computers. By claiming that turf, I could stay in New York, and make videos for field offices. My staff does the traveling."

Because the training field requires an enthusiastic, energetic presence, she projected the image expected of her. Because she looked good, people assumed there was nothing wrong. She could always smile and show an interest in other people no matter what she felt inside. As she said, "I used to think people would see me gritting my teeth, but most of the time they don't know." Often she would drive herself. She was determined to do everything within her power to control her pain, *too* determined. Her body became rigid as she attempted to avoid a painful move, and this added to her stress/pain cycle. Like many Listers and Logicals, she needed to practice letting go and relaxing.

Sometimes remission occurs, but in Beth's case, the arthritis did *not* go away. Eventually, she learned to pace herself, monitoring the pain and trying to avoid too much walking and standing. She did most of her writing at a computer now, and wouldn't even attempt to open a jar with a screw-on lid. She did most of her shopping by catalog to save her energy.

She hadn't planned it this way. None of us do. Like others with chronic conditions, she made the best of it within her limits. She was just one of the thirty-seven million Americans to suffer from arthritis, one out of seven of us.

Even in the face of a health crisis, many individuals forge ahead in their chosen careers. One woman with severe hypertension carries notes about what to do in an emergency wherever she goes. The name of her doctor, her preferred hospital and her medications are all listed. Beth continued in the same career, but scaled back somewhat.

In other instances, illness or an accident throws a career off course. Bosses or clients may not understand or may forget, demanding more than we can fulfill. A young man disabled in an auto accident said his boss still expected him to race through airports, handling luggage and crutches.

After a health crisis, an individual may be falsely perceived as less capable than before. You might find you're overlooked for choice assignments or a promotion because your supervisor sees you differently. Maybe you need to tell your boss or your colleagues, "I'm okay." Working extra hard to *prove* that you're okay could be a serious mistake, though.

Your best bet may be to adjust your career, shift to a department with different demands, ask for less travel, work more flexible hours. Or you could get an early start on the alternate career you'd envisioned for your retirement. Those who survive best when a health crisis stalls one career are those with something else they can do: a backup. Having the attitude of a Learner can help those caught by surprise to treat a bad situation as a challenge to be met.

These bad situations are more likely to occur as we grow older. Even without a specific problem like arthritis, growing older forces people to take the measures Beth has: cutting back on what they do, pacing themselves and grabbing a moment's rest when possible. **You don't have to abandon what you love, just shift how you do it.** Among your contemporaries, you may even be able to chuckle about the tricks that age plays on us. You'll find, though, that your younger friends and your children don't want to hear about aches, pains and diminished capacities. These symptoms are distressing to them, perhaps threatening as well.

Coping with Stress

Even if you are very young and haven't experienced a health crisis, you're no stranger to stress. These are stressful times. Men and women worry about rising prices, job security, city crime, our kids, our parents, etc. Life in any major city can be definitely Domino! Life in the suburbs is much the same with the added stress of a long commute. People plan a vacation, then trouble themselves over air safety and terrorists. Stress is part of life on this planet.

High blood pressure, headaches, backaches, angina, depression, anxiety, insomnia, irritability, excessive drinking, difficulty getting up in the morning, indigestion and being short-tempered are all signs of stress. Stress takes a toll on our bodies and minds. During one particularly harrowing week on Wall Street, one company sent six managers off in ambulances.

All of my original women seemed conscious of stress and took steps to deal with it. Many had moved to jobs or businesses of their own where they were more in control of their stressors. Most had changed their diets and fewer were smoking. Yet one woman said, "The stress was so great I began losing my eyebrows!" Another thought she was having a heart attack during the 1987 stock market crash. It was "only" anxiety.

Women react as strongly as men to stress, but our blood pressure doesn't go up as much, because of estrogen. This is fortunate, because we typically have more stressors, including the tightrope at work and multiple responsibilities at home. Working mothers can't relax at the end of the day and are much more stressed than their mothers were. They may lose sleep, compounding their fatigue.

As professional women, we also drive ourselves. We forget that goals and ambitions take time to achieve. We quicken our pace, take on additional assignments and push ourselves to work long hours. Reaching our goals and securing the promotions we'd hoped for often multiplies the stress. We may not stop until we're literally exhausted or ill in some way. As Claudia Deutsh has noted, there are *darker* sides to women's success—eating disorders, smoking, drug abuse, alcoholism and other self-destructive behavior.

In desperation many women turn to tranquilizers, painkillers, diet pills or even food. Dependency on chemicals can be established very quickly, sometimes while following a doctor's orders to the letter. Tolerances build fast too. Carole found she needed two, then three pain pills for her back pains and finally saw she was in danger of a full-blown addiction. Now she relies on exercise, hot baths and an elastic brace, saving the medication for an emergency.

Alcoholism is rising among women. Even at professional lunches, a few drink too much. Allison noted that one woman, a veteran attorney, got visibly inebriated at a luncheon meeting. "She was supposed to be a role model, but really turned off those young attorneys." More likely, though, a professional woman will conceal her drinking, indulging only after hours, away from work colleagues. Like men drinkers, she'll try to keep her habit from interfering with her job.

Many alcoholics get help when their drinking begins to affect their job performance. In the late eighties, corporations played an important part in pushing people with alcohol or drug problems into treatment, which often leads to recovery. When someone's job is in jeopardy, that person is more likely to change. Even costly inpatient treatment programs don't always work. Sometimes the intervention comes too early, before the person is ready for help. Because of costs, company policies are tougher now, often not offering that second chance after a relapse.

More than a third of Americans will suffer mental or substance-abuse disorders at some time in their lives, reports the National Institute of Mental Health, many before they reach age forty-five. Men have higher rates of substance abuse and violent behavior, while women are higher on anxiety and depression.

What happens often isn't as important ultimately as how we respond. Whether we perceive problems as a Discrete series of hassles or as a Domino disaster makes a difference. Stress has its most destructive impact when you feel that things are beyond your control, as may happen in Domino times. If you're physically fatigued but feel good about what you've done, your body is less likely to have a stress reaction. A brief flare-up of emotions can be worse than fatigue from hard work, one Yale study showed.

Listers and Logicals, who have a greater need for control over various elements of their lives, may suffer greater frustration and greater stress. On the other hand, if they tackle each problem, Discrete fashion, one by one, they may also eliminate stress more easily than Listeners and Leapers, who become overwhelmed by the totality of events. Caught up in volatile periods of change, however, even goal-directed Logicals and Listers found old strategies no longer effective. The process of letting go was quite painful. That's when they sought help. Although some employers have wellness programs with stress-management sessions, we can't wait for our companies to rescue us. With something as important as health, we must initiate action, taking steps on our own.

Our behavior and beliefs have consequences for our health. Knowing what stresses you and why will help you deal with stress more effectively. When you've just undergone a situation that seemed stressful, ask yourself how you would rate it on a scale of one to ten, with ten being the most stressful situation you can imagine. Situations you might rate are meetings with your boss, meetings with difficult colleagues or staff, commuting to and from work, the last five minutes before you leave for work in the morning, the first five when you arrive home at night. One woman with children at home insists on three minutes of absolute silence when she comes in the door. Sometimes changing just a few things in your life gets rid of a lot of stress.

At Overachievers Anonymous, originally organized as Superwomen Anonymous, people learn to say "Enough is enough." **Much of women's stress comes from trying to do too much.** We can learn to say no, not just to drugs, but to excessive demands on our time and our energy. We need to back out when we find ourselves becoming overextended, and start taking care of *ourselves.*

Ask yourself: Do I belong to too many organizations? Do I take on too many extra chores during the holidays? Am I carrying more than my share of the load at home or at work? Practice saying, "I'm sorry but I just don't have time." Look for sources of help and support at home and at work. Later in this chapter, you'll find some suggestions on making changes using the different coping styles.

Realize, if you can, that **things don't have to be perfect.** Your house doesn't have to be spotless, your clothes the latest, your meals made from scratch, your children treated to every lesson or activity. Choose what's most important. Forgive yourself for not achieving the impossible. If you're going to be exhausted, be sure it's from doing something that really matters, or better yet, stop *before* you become exhausted.

Every year research finds new links between the mind and the body. We've seen affirmation, laughter and even smiling as positive forces in recovery from illness, probably because of endorphins produced. Most of us have within our bodies the necessary chemicals to get well and stay well.

New research on success concludes that being able to manage emotions allows us to use our intellectual abilities more effectively. You probably know successful individuals who don't manage their emotions well at all, but they're the exceptions. You're stacking the odds in your favor by staying in charge of your emotions.

It's no surprise that anger or frustration at how they've had to alter their ambitions can put people at risk. The *Wall Street Journal* reported abandonment of the theory of the hard-driving Type A personality as a magnet for heart attacks. New research focuses on those who are disappointed with the way their lives have turned out. A bright thirty-six-year-old man who hated his job as a truck driver complained of chest pains, then suffered a fatal heart attack. A Harvard cardiology professor said that the young man was angry about the "contradiction in his life."

Emotional turmoil in relationships takes its toll on our health and our career potential too, as the women in my research revealed. Divorce has a longer-term effect on all family members, and is the hardest, physically and emotionally, of any life change.

Learning to cope with stress is a necessary competency for professionals in the years ahead. We can avoid some stress, though certainly not all of it. **We can take stock of our priorities and go for the things that matter most.** As women with many demands on our time, we can sidestep the perfectionist trap and say no to some things and some people. We can also get help and support, especially from the people closest to us. The resources that can ease a crisis can also help diminish day-to-day stress in our lives.

TOWARD A HEALTHIER LIFE-STYLE

We must learn to take care of ourselves. Although heredity may leave us predisposed to certain illnesses, we *can* control environmental factors that help trigger them. Managing stress is important, along with watching our diets, getting enough exercise and not smoking. Monitoring such factors as blood pressure and cholesterol levels helps too.

As a professional woman, you may see yourself as too busy to exercise regularly, prepare low-sodium or low-fat meals, make return visits to the doctor or schedule regular checkups. Starting such simple precautions before you're well along in life can make a difference. Studies show that individuals adopt more positive health behaviors as they grow older, but by then these behaviors may have less impact.

Other factors also influence how well we take care of ourselves. Studies at the Institute of Behavioral Sciences at the University of Colorado at Boulder tracked students to see if their health behaviors were connected to their overall philosophy of life. They found that students who avoided risk behaviors and who cared about proper eating and exercise had a more conventional mindset: They respected the rules, valued achievement and placed a low value on independence.

On the other hand, those who took more risks with their health valued independence more than academic achievement, had more relaxed standards of right and wrong, and were generally more rebellious. Those taking more health risks were more like our Leapers while the conventional group resembled the Listers and Logicals.

With breast cancer and cervical cancer, the same measures that decrease the odds of heart attacks can diminish hereditary factors too. Early detection is a big factor in surviving breast or cervical cancer. Regular gynecological exams and Pap smears, examining our own breasts and, over forty, having regular mammograms are crucial.

One woman says, "I feel like a walking time bomb. All the women on both sides of my family have had breast cancer. I go every three months for a checkup." Lister that she was, Beth made appointments for annual checkups on her birthday, so she'd remember every year. Like all of us, she has much more health information and resources than our mothers did.

What does it take to initiate action in changes that are vital to our health and life? Those who are successful in making major life-style changes have something researchers term "self-efficacy," or the confidence needed to produce results. This confidence comes through experience and even some backsliding, so that one eventually knows what works. Failures usually stem from trying too much all at once, and it may take several failures before having a success. But once a person chalks up a success in one area, the mastery can be applied to other areas. **Knowing you've coped with other life changes can help you alter your health habits too.** The Learner in particular profits from her willingness to benefit from mistakes, which contributes to a healthier, more responsible life-style.

Ever conscious of her image, Beth was always neat and conservative in her dress. She collected outfits of wool and silk and linen that set off antique jewelry inherited from women in her family. Yet for a while after her arthritis was diagnosed, Beth couldn't get into her clothes.

"I was on the road a lot, so I had cortisone shots to stay mobile. With each shot, I put on another five pounds! I tried diets I read about, but they left me without energy or feeling ill. I finally hit a hundred and sixty, and decided to get help."

A friend suggested a nutrition center that medically supervised a low-calorie diet. Beth was so determined she even signed on at a health club. "The exercise machines were killing my joints, so I stopped that. But in five months I was back to a hundred and twenty. Whew!"

Meeting her goal boosted her self-esteem and gave her the sense of control she needed. She maintained her normal weight after that by following a specific regimen of food (she has lists for every meal) and supplements too. Her restored image enabled her to think of pursuing new ambitions as a consultant in her field. She made it clear that she's not obsessive about weight, however. "I want to be the best I can be. That goes for everything, and that's what I tell people in my role as a training professional—be the best you can."

After changing her eating habits, Beth could see and feel the results.

Just one change altered her point of view on her health and on her future too. A number of my interviewees also enrolled in group-nutrition and weight-loss programs. They weren't trying to be fashion-plate thin but they knew the health risks and they believed that their weight held them back professionally. Achieving their goal of losing a set number of pounds was more satisfying than they'd imagined and spurred them on to try new things.

Several women in my research also smoked, although well aware of the hazards. Guilt over unhealthy habits usually isn't sufficient motivation to stop. Even a thorough knowledge of the dangers of smoking rarely makes a difference. Smoking is an addiction and, some say, one of the hardest to kick. Fear tactics are almost no help. The desire for social approval or to look and feel better may motivate some.

One woman, definitely a Listener, tried to stop several times and finally did so in a program with weekly meetings. She went out of curiosity and in hopes of meeting new people. "I don't recall ever deciding not to smoke. I enjoyed the company and the meetings, and let myself be swept along. I followed the instructions, gradually learning to enjoy not smoking," she says. She hasn't smoked in nine years. Listeners and other women too may find the support of a group helps in altering life-style and behavior patterns.

Regular exercise is important to health too. A Lister or Logical may have the discipline for solitary exercise; Listeners and Leapers want to be with people or otherwise make it fun. Besides exercise, health clubs and country clubs also offer social and business contacts. Schools with adult classes may offer various sports as well as stretching, yoga and T'ai Chi, the Chinese exercise often practiced by older people. Walking is increasingly popular even as safe places to walk become scarcer; some suburbanites take to the malls. A professional woman on a tight schedule may have a personal trainer who finds what exercises are best for her, then sees that she does them. Excellent videocassettes exist and some women give high priority to using them, setting aside a certain time each day. Some read or watch TV while pedaling their exercise bikes. In time, exercising becomes a break they look forward to.

Overall well-being contributes to health and longevity too. Rosalind Barnett, Grace Baruch and Caryl Rivers in *Lifeprints* found no *one* life-style best for women; each had its pluses and minuses. A sense of mastery combined with supportive personal relationships was key, however. Combining home and work roles gave a sense of pride *if* one did not strive for perfection.

A Roper poll showed that influential people in our society, if given more hours in a day, would spend the time reading, on hobbies, fixing their homes and being with their families and friends—all the Listener aspects that may be missing in their hours at work. In lieu of having more hours, you *can* commit yourself to a life-style with time for the things that matter. Don't put them off. Give yourself those pleasure breaks in the course of *every* week as Beth learned to do.

Stop and look around you, at your living space. Is it serene, comforting, healthful? Can you relax and escape the outside world? Is it cluttered, unsafe, lacking fresh air? Our surroundings can have an indirect but very real influence on us. Some contemporary designers employ ancient Oriental ideas known as Feng Shui to arrange uncluttered living spaces with a subliminal calming effect. Moving to a new home can make a difference too, as women reported. Look at your neighborhood and your community. Some people are active in their communities, working with others to make the changes they want. By working with the less advantaged, Carole added a sense of peace *and* purpose to her life, as did Allison with her environmentalist interests. Think about what you can change to enhance your existence.

A valuable psychological skill for your mental well-being is projecting yourself into the future and envisioning the possibilities awaiting you. People focused on the past or the present lack the broader lifespan perspective that lets them see both backward and forward in their lives. An orientation toward the future can impel you to be aggressive about promotions, to earn money for the future and to guard your health zealously too. Future focus is one of the competencies we'll look at in the next chapter.

As you may have secretly suspected, a sense of humor counts for plenty too. A Boston University study found a connection between humor and problem solving. People with a sense of humor showed themselves to be better workers, wiser and with a broader perspective. Researchers found the most productive workers are the ones who have the most fun on their jobs. They're more relaxed, less bored, more creative, have fewer conflicts with co-workers and enjoy the social bonding humor brings about. Seeing the humor in the antics of her kids and the soap-opera lives of her friends, Diana found that it eased tension too. Why not take the time to relax and have fun again?

Finally, commitment and intense concentration help us by generating euphoric states of mind. How time flies when we're absorbed in a challenging task! "Peak performance" is what author Charles A. Garfield calls it. Athletes have recognized for some time a state of almost effortlessness when we're energized and performing at our best. Hobbies may also absorb us this way. Try to devote more time to whatever activities give you this feeling. Your health will be better for it.

Whatever unleashes our power and sets our energy in motion, we must relish and pursue. **Changes that can make our lives better as well as longer are within our reach.** The resources and the planning techniques that enhance careers can make a difference in your health and overall well-being too. The following exercises will help you apply what you've learned to your own situation and schedule some important actions into your busy life.

EXERCISE I

YOUR LIFE-STYLE ASSESSMENT

1. Think about the changes you would like to make in your behavior or with the items and situations below.

ITEM	CHANGES NEEDED	ACTIONS TO TAKE
Overall health		
Stressors		
Family		
Friends		
Finances		
Work-Related		
Environment		
Clutter		
Nutrition		
Fitness/Exercise		
Weight Control		
Smoking/Drinking		
Drug Abuse		
Mental Health		
Medical Checkups		

Coping Strategies   _____   _____
Other   _____   _____

2. Get out your calendar and set a date for starting and completing each action you plan to take. Schedule at least one important step for tomorrow at the latest. Don't procrastinate. But don't be discouraged if you don't succeed immediately. Keep trying until you find what works for you.

YOUR HEALTH AND AMBITIONS

1. Think of the times in your past when a personal or family illness has altered your ambitions. List the name and illness of each person in turn.

   _____

   _____

2. What future health problems of yours (or of someone you know) might alter your ambitions? _____

   _____

   _____

3. What can you do to prepare or to retain more of a sense of control should this (these) event(s) happen? List the actions you can take. _____

   _____

   _____

PROGRESS REPORT

Increasing your awareness and understanding how your health, your style and ambitions interact is the first step toward positive change. If you've begun to adopt a different perspective on your health, as our five women did, you've started taking charge of another key area of your life.

Allison said, "Some things are so unfair. My father's illness makes me feel helpless, but there's no sense in making myself sick too. Keith and I have stepped up our hiking lately, which seems to give us even more energy for the business we're starting."

Beth echoed what she'd said earlier. "You *can* work around chronic pain. And you *can* lose weight and feel wonderful afterward. Believe me, it's worth it." She had filed away articles on menopause, weight loss, heart attacks and aging parents as well as her own medical records to have the facts should she need them. She added that she was investigating private health and disability insurance that she'd need if she became self-employed. "I've been turned down by several companies, but I understand others might take me if they could exclude coverage for preexisting illnesses," she said. Illness is another factor that makes job changing harder.

Carole took up yoga. "I was looking for something that would keep my back muscles from going into painful spasms. Some yoga stretches are just what I needed. Now I'm getting into the spiritual aspect of yoga. It's very centering, very quieting. It really helps with stress and gives me a sense of harmony with the rest of the world." She sat in a semi-lotus posture with a smile as contented as any Buddha. She told me she'd developed a taste for vegetarian cooking too.

"My early scare with cancer taught me not to take anything for granted," Diana recalled. "I get more out of each day now. Also, we've set up trusts for our children. Meanwhile, Nate and I are watching what we eat. I'm sure we'd all be healthier without the junk food in our kitchen. I can pull the healthiest from each tradition. . . . Stick around for a kosher burrito!"

"That's it," Elinor said as she snuffed out her cigarette. "I have *got* to get in better condition. Look at these yellow fingers and teeth! Everyone says things taste better when you give up smoking. Maybe there's a spa I can afford? Do an image workshop in exchange for a freebie? Who can I call?" Her fingers leapt to her Rolodex. Would it take this time? Who knew?

As you shape the future you want for yourself, health is an important component in your planning, perhaps the single most important. It can also be the least predictable. When health changes come, they affect every area of our lives. Other women have coped, however, and you too can learn your way through health challenges to achieve real well-being. While being a Learner doesn't guarantee good health, it opens up a willingness to try new approaches, build on past experiences and face the future with optimism.

No, we don't know, can't know what's ahead, but we can become individuals who not only survive, but who more effectively play whatever cards we're dealt. The last part of the book focuses specifically on planning for whatever happens in your future, by helping you build your career competencies, decide if change is in order and put it all together in a plan to get you there.

PART III

PLANNING YOUR FUTURE

As you started this book, I asked if your life had turned out differently from what you'd expected. Most likely it has, and you've probably been thinking about how you've altered your ambitions along the way. Undoubtedly there will be more surprises ahead too.

Through the first two parts of the book, you've been gearing up toward planning for a future in which you'll have more of the things you want even as things around you keep changing. In the first part of the book, you became familiar with the different coping styles and with the necessity for becoming more situational and flexible in the years ahead. You saw how other women have coped with various types of change and you were introduced to resources to tap for help. In Part II, you considered the overall shape of your career, and how relationships and health also affect ambitions. You probably now have a sense of the overall shape you want your future to take.

What's next in your life? The last three chapters of the book will guide you through specific career-planning steps. First you'll look at specific competencies for the years ahead and how they relate to the different coping styles. Then you'll have a chance to consider whether or not to make a career or life-style change. Finally, you'll be putting it all together in a flexible yet workable plan for your future.

CHAPTER VII

Career-Building
Competencies

THE world is asking more of us. The arena in which we compete for jobs, promotions and clients is more demanding all the time. Whom you know, where you studied, even where you worked yesterday are less important than what you can do today and tomorrow.

Competencies are what you can do. They're talents, skills and expertise that you can demonstrate. Earlier I mentioned some general competencies or skills that go along with each of the coping styles.

The competencies we'll discuss in this chapter, however, are the talents, skills and expertise that show in your career achievements. They combine talents you were born with and skills you acquire. They're the building blocks of your career. Perhaps you organized a marketing campaign or introduced managers to new technology. Certain competencies lie behind these and other accomplishments on your résumé, and they're your future potential too. **Proven competencies are what employers (and clients) look for, what you get paid for, and what advances your career.**

Each field has its own specific competencies. As you move from intern to supervisor to manager to director, you add new levels of expertise. To advance, you must show that you are above average—in fact, highly capable in your area of expertise.

The competencies we'll be talking about here, however, are trans-

159

ferable from profession to profession, cutting across all fields. They're assets that help you change jobs, even change careers. They'll also help you in building the relationships, health and life-style you want. Your use of these competencies and your increasing awareness of important trends will help you position yourself strategically for the future.

They relate to the five basic coping styles: Logical, Lister, Listener, Leaper and Learner, although there's some overlapping. You have some in your repertoire already. As you go along, note the ones you will need to strengthen in order to reach your goals.

LOGICAL COMPETENCIES

1. **Critical thinking** means examining assumptions—yours and everybody else's—finding the hidden agendas, asking who's grinding what ax. **It's looking behind what someone is saying to discover what they have to gain, what their biases are.**

We often assume other people are much like ourselves in their values and motivations. In reality, people are very different. Some always put money first, for example. Others invariably worry if anybody will get hurt. Some care what other people will think and some don't. Don't just assume someone will react in a certain way.

Be critical too of what you read or learn through the media. What is the purpose—to entertain, to inform or to sway your thinking? What are the sources of information? Is the research identified? Is the authority cited reputable? Does more than one reputable authority agree? Don't be afraid to dismiss certain things as baloney. Allison did and impressed her bosses.

Practice thinking critically by analyzing announcements during a political campaign. Look for the difference between image and substance. Go beneath that surface. Dig for the truth beneath the trivia.

Thinking critically means using your intellect, stretching your brain as you did in your toughest college course or work assignments. Some people who stay in a job for a long time let their critical abilities get soft. Interviewers, however, want to see how you think and may throw you a problem to test you.

For Allison, wrestling with mental challenges and questioning what she read or heard began at her family dinner table when she was very young. She'd say, "Yes, but . . ." a lot and has had to stop herself when her impulse was to criticize, which could be hard on relationships.

Listeners, always more trusting, may go with their feelings, which is just what a shrewd manipulator intends. Leapers, bored by technical discussion, jump to conclusions *without* all the facts.

2. **Thought catching** keeps your perspective realistic. Many people tend to make catastrophes out of mere calamities. The language we use conversationally encourages this. We say we're having a disaster when we're just having a problem.

Cognitive therapy encourages catching ourselves when we magnify our negative thoughts, saying "There I go again," then restating the thought, "I may not *like* being fired, but this is *not* Armageddon. I *can* deal with it."

Beth was the one to leave her alcoholic husband and file for divorce. Afterward, though, she was particularly hard on herself, accepting the blame for the breakup of the marriage and even for *his* drinking. "I'd told him that I'd leave him if he didn't quit—why didn't he? I thought that meant something was wrong with me. I carried the weight of the world on my shoulders. After I'd been in Al-Anon for a while, I learned that he had made a choice. Now I can catch myself when those thoughts reappear and I start to assume responsibility for things that aren't mine to decide." Thought catching takes practice, but can save a lot of grief.

Thought catching came naturally to Allison. Beth, as a Lister, learned the process and made it one of her major competencies to use in facing any problem. Leapers and Listeners find it more difficult but especially need it when they're in a torrent of Domino changes.

3. **Financial savvy.** Even if your specialty has little to do with the financial side of a company, the better you understand it, the more valuable you'll be to an organization. Be very careful with numbers if you're not used to them. Nothing is more embarrassing than saying "million" when you meant "billion," and it could be worse than embarrassing. Yet some people get bamboozled by all the zeros.

If the jargon of finance is alien to you, get help from a friend or associate. Your résumé will be more impressive too if you say, "managed $1 million ad budget," instead of simply "responsible for ad budget."

Before agreeing to take a job, analyze the financial condition of the company. If it's a public company, get a copy of its annual report, look at the debt/equity ratio, also find out what financial analysts and others in the industry are saying. In a private company, ask questions during your interviews and get outside opinions too.

Women who face glass ceilings in blue-chip companies can sometimes get higher-level or increased responsibility in companies that are in financial trouble or in turnaround status. Is the experience worth the chance of being out of work? It might be a real coup to add it to your résumé. But assess the risk carefully. If you need security at this stage in your career, as Elinor did, don't board a sinking ship. Elinor looked at the image her company presented, not the balance sheet. **Many a career has been waylaid because financials weren't investigated.**

We all need financial savvy in a personal sense as well, to make the most of the financial resources we have. This means analyzing our expenses and projecting what we're going to need in the future based on alternative scenarios. Be ready for that financial emergency like Elinor's. Over seventy percent of young professionals like her are in financially poor shape for retirement and have difficulty saving, reports the *Wall Street Journal*. At any stage we need a cushion for emergencies, "I quit" money or an alternate source of income.

Also, measure personal decisions according to their cost/benefit ratio. Understand how to make credit work for you by careful borrowing for major acquisitions and how it can work against you by letting you think you're far richer than you are.

Over the years, keep building equity for your retirement and other late-life goals. If you've changed jobs a lot or are self-employed, this is your *own* responsibility. The money you earn must do more than "tide you over" for now; some should be put aside for the future. Stay up to date on what options the IRS allows on your retirement funds.

Books or software on personal finance can help you map out your personal strategies. If you're like most busy professionals whose fields aren't related to investing, you'll need to rely on an expert such as a well-reputed financial planner or stockbroker. But you'll still need to be knowledgeable about investments you make. Ideally, your relationship with a financial expert will increase your financial savvy as well as your net worth.

4. **Computer and technological literacy** are essential in *any* field these days. **Studies show that men are way ahead of women in being receptive to new technology.** So if you're not the first to know the new

technologies in your field, don't be the last. Find out what the leaders in your field are saying in their seminars or writing in their articles. When you don't understand something, read up on it or enroll in a class.

Use of a computer gives you access to much more information, and can put you in a more powerful position. Whether or not you have a computer terminal on your desk, be aware of how computers are reshaping the way your company functions and your customers' businesses have changed. Don't miss a chance to be involved with new technologies in the course of your job. On your résumé, list how you've used new equipment and systems to benefit your company.

Beth and Allison took to computers like fish to water. Diana mastered word processing, although Listeners and Leapers are more likely to be technophobes. Elinor liked computer games, which are a step toward the spread sheets she'll eventually need to project the earnings of her own business. Carole made sure her bank's automatic tellers were "user friendly."

5. **Analysis of trends and facts** coming into your world is essential too. **You need to understand how they relate to *your* life and career.** The Introduction covered the major trends that currently affect large numbers of us—demographic, economic, global, technological and social. Others may have a more direct impact on you. New ones are emerging every day. You'll get a chance to factor these trends into your planning at the end of this chapter.

Meanwhile, annual issues of *Forbes, Fortune, Business Week*, among others, have profiles of movers and shakers by industry. Note what their achievements and problems are. Other publications have year-end issues summarizing changes and trends. Stay current with media both in and outside your field. This probably means reading specialized publications and, selectively, at least one major daily newspaper. Perhaps the *Wall Street Journal* or *Christian Science Monitor* is necessary for your field.

Looking at sources for trends and then assessing them is called environmental scanning. Allison was doing this as part of her growing interest in pollution and toxic waste control. She still kept abreast of legal issues, but added literature from the Sierra Club and the Green movement and emerging biotech solutions to her knowledge base.

Listers go about scanning for trends in an organized way. Listeners like

Diana need to link this process with people and other elements that interest them. Leapers like Elinor may be less aware of certain trends not related to their interests, yet their intuitive abilities enable them to scan a lot of complex information and synthesize key factors.

LISTER COMPETENCIES

1. **Information management** means being on top of what's happening so that you can discuss innovations in interviews and implement them in your job. This competency goes along with analyzing trends. Many people find they need to manage the information before they can analyze it.

You're not alone if you feel overwhelmed by everything bombarding you from the mail and the media, computer data bases, phone and fax. Learn to skim, take a speed-reading course, subscribe to a service that summarizes business books, read the reviews or buy books on tape.

Beth used her circular file when opening her mail, looking at each piece only once, not even opening the junk mail. You don't *have* to, either. A secretary or assistant who knows your priorities can be a godsend, especially in seeing that things don't get into a logjam when you're away.

Beth read the tables of contents in journals and newspapers, then glanced at the headlines and the first paragraphs of stories. She clipped key items to read in a spare moment, carrying them with her for commuter reading, but she didn't read every word. "I get the gist, and move on," she said.

Use your VCR to record important programs or to watch videos that keep you up to date. Listen to a good public radio news broadcast as you commute.

Trade off reading with friends. You cover certain journals, they cover others. Clip or copy articles of interest for each other. Note quickly if an article adds something new or if it's just a rehash of old information.

If you're between jobs or at home temporarily for any reason, keep your professional journals coming. The time Diana was recuperating from surgery put her ahead professionally. Go to professional meetings too, if you can, to hear what's happening in your field, touch base with colleagues and keep your network alive. Diana stayed in phone contact with colleagues. You might also get tapes of meetings. Keep up to date so you can hit the ground running!

2. **Time and life management** mean making the most of the years, months, weeks and days you have, achieving the balance you want between work and other parts of your life. Decide what's important, then organize your life to make time for it.

Life planning has been around since the days of Aristotle. The Greeks made seven-year plans. Many of us today think in five-year segments. David Campbell says if you don't know where you're going, you just might end up there! Granted, sixty percent of executives surveyed by Korn Ferry began their careers without clear goals. Once you're in a career, however, goals are a means of charting your direction and marking each milestone.

Some say being prepared to take advantage of the opportunities when they come is a form of luck. You can help make your *own* luck by checking your progress on a regular basis. Even if your five-year career and life plan looks achievable now, you need to assess where you are annually or more often.

Try looking at your situation every six months and asking, "Is this turning out as I'd hoped? If not, what can I do to change the situation? Is it time to move on?" The next chapter will help you look at your options for changing.

Next, set a specific goal for each six-month period, such as acquiring a skill (or one of these competencies), learning a body of information, completing a project, all in addition to your normal mix of activities. Over the years, the skills, courses and projects can really add up.

To get more out of each day, high-tech office equipment can be as liberating for us as the automatic washing machine and dishwasher were for earlier generations. **Work smarter, not longer.** Take advantage of modems, fax machines, voice and electronic mail to communicate more efficiently and to get more done in the time you have. Telecommuting lets working mothers spend more time with their families. The beeper and the car phone keep you in touch with work on the one hand and the baby-sitter and home on the other.

There are hundreds of courses and books, even consultants, on time management, life and career planning and organizing your life. Some of my favorites are listed in the resource section at the end of this book.

Whatever your time and life needs, have it *your* way. Negotiate a more flexible schedule, if you need to. Cite the examples you've seen in the business press. If you want to start your own business, you *must* stick to schedules and deadlines, establish priorities, weigh options, make decisions—all Lister skills. Listeners and Leapers may need to force themselves to structure their lives. Diana was often late until she thought about how this inconvenienced others. She started doing better, though, organizing her calendar and scheduling time for creative writing in her busy life. Elinor would forget what time it was, but she did have future plans.

3. **Gaining control** in order to manage effectively no longer means ruling with an iron fist and imposing your will upon others. One reason is that so many more individuals now have access to information. If you're a manager, this calls for prioritizing duties and organizing projects as Listers do so well. In addition, you delegate more authority to staff members, and share power with them too. You may even supervise staff members you rarely see because they're at home or on the road, or you may work with "leased" employees or independent contractors.

This competency entails blending Lister organizing skills with Listener skills for communicating, and above all, for motivating. It draws on the various different coping styles. Gaining control in this new era actually means relinquishing *rigid* control in the old sense. **Those who are too rigid or who have difficulty tolerating risk or ambiguity must learn to let go.** Those who take refuge in "the way we always did it" will be out of touch.

4. **Managing change** calls on *all* coping abilities, but it's often Listers who are charged with implementing change in their companies. They decide what comes first and structure the progression of changes, whether introducing a new phone system or downsizing a company. They gain the support of workers at different levels, sell the ideas and sometimes eliminate jobs.

Lister skills combine with Listener skills to facilitate change in organizations. There may be many variables, many occurrences stimulating the need for change. There may also be many people whose lives are involved and many resisting it, each for different reasons.

Increasingly companies are relying on trained specialists in change from the field of organization development (O.D.), who may be part of the human resource department team. They consult with managers in different departments and divisions of a company to implement changes. In marketing bank services, Carole worked with specialists to foresee such things as consumer resistance to automatic tellers and strategize how to gain consumer acceptance for various forms of electronic banking.

A summary of such achievements is highly impressive on a résumé. Logicals as well as Listers can also chart the process of change effectively. Listeners bring people skills to the process and are especially helpful during personnel cutbacks and other changes that trigger strong emotions. Leapers' ability to imagine the future can play an important role here too.

LISTENER COMPETENCIES

1. **Self-management** competencies entail an acute awareness of your own behavior—its consequences and how it affects others. It includes understanding your beliefs and values, as well as how you've been socialized differently from others. **It also means coping with setbacks and events beyond your control, maintaining your self-esteem and managing your own emotions.** Underlying it may be an overall purpose or sense of direction to your life in terms of social consciousness or spirituality.

Self-management is an overall maturity and wisdom that comes with experience. As the women in my research repeatedly pointed out, mastering the major events of their lives gave them new insights and understanding of themselves and others.

Self-management didn't come easily to Elinor, but therapy and personal-growth seminars helped. "I used to fly off the handle like a spoiled brat when I didn't get my way. I must have been hard to take," said Elinor. Understanding others begins with yourself, as Elinor found.

You can speed up the process by attending workshops such as National Training Labs groups or The Center for Creative Leadership's "Looking Glass." Logicals and Listeners may be more in touch with their emotions after such an experience. Some individuals, especially Listeners, welcome constructive feedback from subordinates, colleagues and superiors on how to be more effective, and take it to heart.

2. **Relationships management** means getting along with your boss, subordinates and peers, and with individuals outside your job too. Since many demands conflict, we need to compromise, negotiate, resolve conflicts in a win/win manner. These are Listener skills but often are all the

more effective if presented in a structured way using Logical abilities too.

Managing relationships means realizing that they cannot be taken for granted: They take work and are always changing. Diana demonstrated the empathic side of relationship management well but needed help in honing her Logical skills. Logical Allison could structure convincing arguments, but needed to be more sensitive to other people's feelings.

3. **Communication and influence skills** include writing proposals, reports and letters, as well as speaking publicly, making presentations and interviewing.

When you don't have direct authority over people, yet must depend on them to get things done, these skills are key. You must communicate your ideas clearly, sell them and get others to "buy in." Carole needed to have influence because direct power over customers and branch managers was no longer feasible. She was persuasive, diplomatic and had the ability to build coalitions. These are effective political skills too.

You know the importance of these if you're in sales, public relations or any field that involves wide contact with people. **In most large organizations, you must employ influence skills in making yourself and your ideas visible so that you'll be singled out for advancement.** In politics or social causes, building coalitions and selling your ideas to others is crucial. Sometimes you're persuading like-minded individuals. Often, though, the challenge is to convince rivals.

With the multicultural environment we're increasingly exposed to, being fluent in other languages can be an advantage too. Diana found the Spanish she learned from her father useful. If you don't have time to study a language, try learning more about the cultures with which you deal. Diana made a point of learning about Asian cultures, and drew upon her ability to "read" people in subtle ways. Understanding gestures, body language, mealtime practices or do's and don'ts for women can go a long way in bridging cultural gaps. Elinor's intuitive ability often compensated for lack of vocabulary in foreign languages when traveling.

4. **Issues management** is valuable in many careers. As a trainer, for example, Beth had to be tuned to worldwide events and be able to identify which issues would have an impact on the workplace generally, her industry and her company. Early on, she zeroed in on sexual harassment,

AIDS in the workplace and age discrimination. Making them her "turf" in her company, she developed policies and programs around them.

In her communications job, Diana picked up on areas of concern to employees such as child-care benefits and health-care policies. Presenting the financial impact to her boss and the humane benefits to employees, she balanced social concerns and the company's bottom-line interests.

Effective issues management begins with spotting the pertinent issues and understanding the role they play. Some Logical analysis of trends and environmental scanning helps here too, as well as the Lister skills of managing change. The final and most important steps are communicating the issues and taking action on them. That action can be a real feather in your cap. Highlight it on your résumé and make sure people know about it.

5. **Participative management** calls for a new kind of leadership. What's required is an ability to motivate and empower people at different levels. As employees are more likely to be organized into democratic units, often with blurred boundaries between jobs, you may be more a facilitator than a boss. Your job now is drawing out the contributions of everyone and inspiring cooperation. You also encourage innovation and creativity, perhaps also trying to achieve consensus instead of using authoritarian or even majority rule. **Participative management means sharing power, and actually empowering others to make decisions and be autonomous.**

Many of the old adversarial workplace relationships are disappearing, replaced by a spirit of cooperation between different levels and functions in a company. A more democratic management style takes more time, especially at the beginning, but many experts believe the increased input yields better decisions. You may also save time in the end by reducing resistance to change and by nipping problems early before they have a chance to hit the grapevine. Employees have an added incentive to do their best and to remain loyal too.

At Diana's personal-care company, the product managers listened to new product ideas from the sales force and took suggestions from their customers. Her communications unit eventually offered more cross-training and greater flexibility with job responsibilities. The individual contributors were now less isolated, and they were all involved in meeting the unit's goals.

Other companies give employees a stake through profit sharing and employee-ownership plans or through bonuses tied to productivity. Not all companies are there yet, but if you'd like to work in such a setting, start by sharing responsibility with your own staff and keep track of the results.

LEAPER COMPETENCIES

1. **Thinking globally and strategically** means widening your perspective, anticipating vital trends and taking action on them. As a woman, your odds of getting an international assignment are less, but wherever you are, international developments have an impact on your career.

Leapers know the world is not a simple, logical place, and they have no wish to make it that way. They not only tolerate, but thrive on the chaos, uncertainty, discontinuity and complexity that are part of reality. While others tremble or panic, they step back, see the big picture and smile at the absurdity of it all. Then they synthesize their strategies and take action while others are still catching up. **This is the major difference between managers, who must focus on a smaller arena, and executives, who *must* see the bigger picture, think conceptually and have a vision of what could be and what it takes to get there.**

Leapers more seasoned than Elinor are skilled entrepreneurs and top executives who "position" themselves and their companies effectively. With maturity and experience, Logicals, Listers and Listeners find it easier to see the big picture and live with ambiguity.

2. **Future focus** is a facet of thinking globally and strategically. **It means thinking ahead and envisioning different future scenarios.** This goes beyond plotting out the logical consequences; it's visualizing many possibilities, even remote ones. Be careful about sharing your future view in an employment interview, however; it's far better to show evidence of a vision that paid off, such as a new product that became a hit.

Elinor was developing these competencies as she sought out new products and dreamed up ways to market them. She had a broad view of her future possibilities, but she needed to hone in on one or two, adopting some sound strategies to get where she wanted to be.

Being able to project yourself into the future is a coping and career-planning skill too. Logicals and Listers may need to remind themselves to dream a little more and to picture how the trends that they analyze and manage can affect them. Being able to focus on the future along with thinking strategically greatly enhances your ability to formulate ambitions for yourself. Achieving them also entails risk taking.

3. **Taking risks** involves a mind-set that's always weighing the probable rewards against the probable *and* possible costs. Anyone can take a risk, but risking and then coming out a winner means drawing on other competencies too, such as critical thinking and financial savvy. Being a successful entrepreneur or a high-ranking executive entails understanding the risks of your field, and knowing when to hold back and when to stake your reputation on something you believe in.

Part of the job of calculating a risk is knowing the worst that can happen and planning how you'd deal with it. Losing money for your company or going belly-up in business doesn't necessarily erode your reputation as, for example, trying to bend the law could.

Most types of failure won't kill you or your career. Underlying a healthy risk-taking attitude is self-esteem. You can take risks if you know that you can pick yourself up from failure and still be good at whatever you do.

If you're not a Leaper, taking risks may not be easy for you. Before you take big ones, practice taking small ones. Keep reaching further, accepting new challenges. Document your bigger "wins" in your résumé and talk about them too.

4. **Creativity and innovation** differentiate the leaders from the followers. Individuals as well as companies are identified by their new ideas. **Effective executives aren't defenders of the status quo.** They know that new challenges demand new solutions. Innovators thrive on change and challenges. They're good at reframing problems and visualizing solutions. They mentally rehearse alternatives. They like the "aha's" of discovery and they continually strive for them.

People who aren't Leapers have creativity too, but it may be dormant. Remember when you were a new employee with a new idea every minute? If your own idea stream has dried up, look for ways to prime it. Have your company send you to Ned Herrmann's Applied Creative Thinking workshops in North Carolina or Synectics in Boston or take a course in creativity for businesspeople. Take up a new hobby—kite flying, finding wildflowers, painting in watercolors. Spend some time with youngsters, if you don't already, and if you do, spend more time away from them to give your own thoughts free reign.

Does creativity flourish in your company's culture? Are your competitors seen as more creative? If you're a Leaper, you've probably left uncreative environments, as most of the Leapers in my research did. If you aren't a Leaper yourself, invite some to join your group. They're good to have around, especially when you're planning major changes. Their humor and enthusiasm fires up everybody else.

Logical and Lister managers may have difficulty communicating with creative staff members and creating an atmosphere where they can generate their best ideas. Creative people generally want less supervision, yet you may find that you have to impose some structure. They usually need benchmarks that are different from those of other employees, and they may need more encouragement and positive feedback too.

LEARNER COMPETENCIES

Learner competencies cut across all others and can be combined and matched with them in ways that make the parts a stronger whole.

1. **Being situational** is the key competency of the Learner. Effective managers and executives are all switch-hitters who use not only the skills but the competencies of the other four styles. **Situational abilities are increasingly important in coping with change and communicating with many different people.** We've seen how Carole's flexibility served her well in her banking career and with personal upheavals as well.

Her balance of abilities made her especially adept at the competencies involving more than one coping skill. She did well managing change, a Lister competency. Her Listener ability to draw people out in participative management was strong too. So was her Leaper capacity for thinking globally and strategically. She needed to work on being able to take bigger risks, yet another Leaper capacity.

Your situational competencies can be hard to demonstrate when you're applying for a job. Don't underrate them, though. The results are evident in the variety of achievements listed on your résumé and in your ease at handling the interview.

2. **Lifelong learning and knowledge expansion** come naturally to people who are achievers in their fields. **Knowledge is power,** after all,

and this was never more true than now, in the information age. **Employers see your expertise as a competitive weapon in their human resource arsenal.** Advanced degrees are increasingly important, and on your résumé or letter of introduction, they usually signal that you have intelligence and knowledge to spare.

But the competency I'm talking about here goes beyond traditional classroom knowledge. It's an attitude that keeps certain people learning all their lives. Mention something Learners haven't heard of, and they won't be satisfied until they know all about it. They're always curious, always eager for new knowledge, skills and experience. Carole wasn't happy for long after ceasing to learn on the job.

Corporations are becoming "learning enterprises," reports Anthony Carnevale in *The Training & Development Journal*. At one rapidly growing company, thirty-two percent of the managers had less than two years of management experience. They learned on the job—by the seat of their pants and skirts! **Working *pays*, not just in the earnings you take home now but in the income potential you gain from your added skills and achievements. Your options increase and your horizons widen with your work experience.**

Notice how you learn best. Is it by doing and experiencing? Or by reading, hearing, seeing, underlining, note taking? Do you get more from discussions, through stories, seeing models, hearing theories, interpreting, researching, exploring, interacting, problem solving? Make it easy for yourself when you have something difficult to master. Notice too what distracts you from learning—procrastination, noise, boredom, fatigue? Ask for help or cooperation from others in eliminating the barriers. Reward yourself as you go along and make it fun.

3. **Complexity, wisdom, judgment, maturity, autonomy and integrity** come as time passes and life events pile up. All of my interviewees described changing in these areas. **Our individual memories include rich histories that color our dealings with the world. Each life has its texture, multipatterned like a tapestry with a design all its own.**

None of these is more important than integrity. Integrity doesn't necessarily come with adult turf, but it's expected in most quarters. Korn Ferry and Columbia University, surveying over 1,500 executives in thirty countries, found that ethics is a top characteristic sought in leaders. The betrayal of a trust may be the kiss of death for a career.

Some women found themselves in conflict with the ethics of their bosses, their companies or their professions, as Allison did. She questioned the ethics of some lawyers and of her company's environmental policies.

Our autonomy, wisdom, judgment, complexity and maturity as well as our self-concepts continue to evolve as long as we live. Although interests, perspectives and values may change with experience, certain themes recur. Reading this book and, in particular, doing the exercises will help you see elements of continuity in your life. **Ultimately, the goal is a sense of mastery, and being at peace with who we are, doing what matters to us, not someone else. Being ourselves is better than having it all.**

EXERCISE I

YOUR CAREER-BUILDING COMPETENCIES

1. Considering the trends most likely to affect your future, check the competencies below that you'll need to advance in your career or to enhance your résumé or life-style.

	ONE OF YOUR STRENGTHS	NEED TO DEVELOP
Logical Competencies		
Critical Thinking	_____	_____
Thought Catching	_____	_____
Financial Savvy	_____	_____
Computer and Technological Literacy	_____	_____
Analysis of Trends and Facts	_____	_____
Lister Competencies		
Information Management	_____	_____
Time and Life Management	_____	_____
Gaining Control	_____	_____
Managing Change	_____	_____

Listener Competencies

Self-Management _____ _____
Relationships Management _____ _____
Communication and _____ _____
   Influence Skills _____ _____
Issues Management _____ _____
Participative Management _____ _____

Leaper Competencies

Thinking Globally _____ _____
   and Strategically _____ _____
Future Focus _____ _____
Taking Risks _____ _____
Creativity and _____ _____
   Innovation _____ _____

Learner Competencies

Being Situational _____ _____
Lifelong Learning _____ _____
   and Knowledge Expansion _____ _____
Complexity, Wisdom _____ _____
   Judgment, Maturity _____ _____
   Autonomy, Integrity _____ _____
Other _____ _____

2. Now add any other competencies, credentials or certifications that are essential for advancement in your field or to attain your five-year goal. ____

_____

_____

3. Prioritize them in order of their importance to your present career. Note future achievements that will demonstrate these competencies. Fill in target dates for those achievements.

PROGRESS REPORT

Certain generic competencies cut across fields. These competencies enhance your employability and your ability to position and market yourself more strategically. They're linked with the trends already identified.

Select those competencies that you believe are most critical to your career and your life. Develop them, hone them and ask others for feedback on how you're doing. By increasing your repertoire, you're arming yourself for whatever change comes, whether it's Discrete or Domino. Not only that, you can define the changes you want to make.

Here's how our five women branched into new competencies as they planned their futures.

"I need to concentrate on innovation and communication for the environmental company Keith and I are going to involve ourselves in," Allison concluded. "We need to think strategically about how to market ourselves and differentiate our services from the competition. We've already begun brainstorming on weekends with two potential partners." She was concentrating on the Leaper and Listener clusters of competencies.

Beth was concentrating on the Logical competencies. Lawry's experience in accounting provided sound financial advice before she acted on her plans.

Carole was focusing on Listener relationships management for a future man in her life, and she was investigating global assignments to improve her Leaper abilities. "I'm concentrating on London. At least I speak the language, so I can focus on learning other things in the financial world there. And it's close to Paris, where Ro can introduce me to those eligible men she keeps writing about. There's method in my madness!"

Diana chose Lister competencies. She found information management helpful in dealing with some highly controversial issues at work, such as using animals for testing. "The company's position has changed radically. First we claimed that these tests were necessary so we wouldn't take undue risks with humans. Now it seems we're stopping these tests entirely." She was also improving her time-management skills and had set long- and short-term goals.

"My real challenge is self-management," Elinor observed. "I'm a little off the wall at times, and it freaks some people out. In a big company, my staff can avoid me, but if I'm going to be in business for myself someday, I've got to get the best from people, not turn them off!" Her Listener concentration would help her not only with staff, but with suppliers, backers and customers too.

Each woman chose the competencies that would move her forward toward her goals. In this chapter, I've asked you too to think strategically about the competencies that will help you achieve the future you want. If you've selected several on which to act, you're on your way.

In the next chapter you'll consider whether or not to make a career or life-style change.

CHAPTER VIII

To Change or
Not to Change?

To change or not? Should you continue along the career track you're traveling, choose a parallel path or veer off in a new direction? Your options depend greatly on how well your career competencies coincide with outside trends. Your choice, ultimately, is much more personal.

In this chapter, we'll first look at the advantages and disadvantages of "staying put" for those who can. We'll also look at making a strategic change and at moving on to a more independent career or business. Maybe you're already in the midst of changes forcing you to take action. Later on in this chapter, we'll consider different life-style options and actions you could take.

CONTINUING THE NEW CLASSIC CAREER

Allison, whose career has been our example of Classic, eventually faced the dilemma of many professionals today. She explained, "I'm earning enough to contribute to my father's nursing-home care as well as our children's college bills. My job is fairly secure too, as long as the company keeps causing environmental disasters. Plenty of legal work in that!

"On the other hand," she held out her palms as if weighing her choices, "How can I live with myself, knowing there's more pollution

178

coming? We can't keep on like this. Companies like ours must start doing things differently. I could be really useful here if policies change, but how long will that take?" She didn't let her colleagues know she'd been volunteering for environmentalist groups. They'd have thought her a traitor.

At forty-five Allison was earning more than she'd ever dreamed of. Outsiders might think she was crazy to consider changing. Anyone employed by a big company who is secure, vested in the company pension plan and enjoying fringe benefits generates this kind of reaction with a suggestion of leaving.

In one survey thirty percent of executives said that up the ladder in a single company was the way to advance a career. But as we've seen in Chapter IV, the ascent up the ladder is more likely to be zigzag than direct. In fact, fifty percent of surveyed executives believe the way to get ahead is a zigzag route—that is, moving from company to company in the same industry.

It's the younger workers who are more likely to change jobs, however. Right now, ninety-two percent of voluntary job changers are under forty-five. As you grow older and become better established in your career, staying in a job is usually safer. If you're a Logical or a Lister, staying where you are is probably more "comfortable" unless upheaval already threatens your security.

Besides weighing your preferences, however, look closely at the career and the job you're in. Is your industry one that keeps on earning in good times and bad? Is your company reasonably safe from a takeover? Is your department essential to the overall growth of the company? Is your contribution appreciated? Is your relationship with your boss good? Is your boss's position secure? If you can answer yes to all of these, staying may be your safest choice, although, as we all know, surprises can happen.

When you've put in a number of years with a company, that job becomes part of your identity. Maybe it's a company with a reputation you're proud of. The longer you've been there, the greater your investment in time and energy. Understandably, you believe that you deserve to reap the rewards—the prestige, the pay raises, benefits and, eventually, a comfortable retirement.

Leapers and Learners, however, seek adventure and challenge. Carole said, "It's torture for me to repeat the same marketing routines over and over. I find myself stirring things up, getting in trouble if I'm bored."

As Carole knew, staying with the same company doesn't and shouldn't mean standing still. Large organizations offer many alternatives, often including international divisions and subsidiaries. Carole was hoping for an assignment at her bank's offices in London.

A transfer to a different part of the United States can also be an antidote to boredom and a chance to learn. If you now work in a branch, spending time at headquarters can stand you in good stead for future opportunities. Going from headquarters to "the field" gives you a better sense of how your company makes its money. Many big companies offer plenty of help with relocation, sometimes even helping to find jobs for the spouses of employees.

Maybe you've put in some time in a staff position, but can transfer to a line job where you'll have a greater impact on profits. On the other hand, you may be in a line slot that you find too narrow. A transfer to staff can give you a broader view of many functions, but because staff jobs are considered an expense to the company, they may be the first to go if a company has to cut back.

Your company may also have subsidiaries or divisions in turnaround or even in start-up status that could test your entrepreneurial abilities. Operating in an ambiguous environment, taking new risks, performing more functions may be just what you need to feel challenged. Your Leaper and Learner competencies are needed here.

Besides developmental assignments, companies may also offer educational opportunities that broaden your experience and help you build your career. Some are university-based advanced-management programs, where you may meet people from other industries and countries and can see how you stack up against others. You'll expand your professional network too. Even if you plan to move to a new job, try to integrate your education with your present job by agreeing on a work-related project or specific goals with your boss. A concrete achievement adds more to your reputation than things you've learned but haven't yet demonstrated.

If there are no outside educational opportunities, find people you can learn from in your company. Select an area or division where you see opportunity and where you think you'd fit. Identify the people you and others admire, then ask to work with them on a project, task force or committee. Carole did this to learn more about real estate and low-income housing while developing new contacts within her company.

Large organizations have many benefits and resources you can tap.

Diana found health and dental policies were a godsend to her family because Nate's family business wasn't able to purchase comparable coverage. She took advantage of flexible hours when the children were ill, and sometimes worked from home; and she always enjoyed the company's social activities for families.

Before deciding to stay or leave, find out what your company offers. Use the following exercise as a reminder of what might be helpful to you at this stage.

EXERCISE I

YOUR ORGANIZATION'S RESOURCES

1. Check the company resources that might be helpful to you now or in the future.

RESOURCE	HELPFUL NOW	FUTURE HELP
Performance Appraisals		
Tuition Refund		
Job Posting		
Training/Workshops		
Retirement Planning		
Employee Assistance		
Internships		
Mentors		
Networks		
Outplacement		
Succession Planning		
Skills Data Bank		
Career Counseling		
Career Info Center		
Job Rotation		
Career Pathing		
Workbooks		
Assessment Centers		
"Cafeteria" Benefits		
Parental Leave		

Child-Care Help   _____   _____
Day-Care Help   _____   _____
Flexible Schedules   _____   _____
Maternity Leave   _____   _____
Relocation Help   _____   _____

Other   _____   _____

2. No company will have all of these resources, but yours may have more than you're aware of. If you're not sure, you may have to do a bit of digging, but check with your Benefits, Training and Employee Assistance people to find out. You may have to make trade-offs or pay for part of some benefits yourself, but "company-sponsored" usually means they're less expensive for you. People who leave large firms cover more of these costs themselves.

A BETTER BALANCE

If you've thought of making a job change yet know it's not your best move, perhaps what you need is a more balanced, varied life in which work no longer dominates your constellation of activities. As Richard Bolles asserts in *The Three Boxes of Life*, life doesn't have to be a sequence of education, followed by work and then finally leisure. A fulfilling life mixes all three concurrently. Involvement with a hobby, charity, new or old family and friends; just enjoying more leisure; or visiting new places can give you fresh energy that carries over to your work life.

Giving back something to your profession can heighten your interest as well as your visibility. Consider mentoring newcomers. You might assume a leadership role in your professional association or serve on its board as preparation for serving on other boards.

You could also pass along things you know in a classroom. With women now making up over fifty percent of college students, you're needed as a role model. You'd be appreciated in ways that are different from work, and you'd certainly learn from your students too. Many companies lend executives to school systems and universities as teaching adjuncts, lecturers and invited speakers. Teaching can also be a route to a future career or part of a diversified package of career activities.

Volunteering is another way to add meaning to your life. Today's volunteers often hold paying jobs too, yet give their time and talent to causes they care about, sometimes totally unrelated to their line of work.

WHEN THE AX IS POISED

Just one factor—a new boss, an industry downturn—can threaten your professional security. With takeovers, mergers and fierce competition in most industries, a job that once looked like a lifetime assignment can be yanked out from under you. Usually, though, there is some warning. **Even with the ax poised to fall, you still have choices.** Maybe your company is being bought and your department is duplicated elsewhere. Maybe you've had a performance review that was negative, and you've been given six months or a year to do something different.

Beth began looking at vendors as possible partners or employers when she heard rumblings of a shakeup in her training department. "The training field is changing and I'm losing ground here," she said. "The company isn't using my strengths anymore. I have less rapport with my new boss, who wants to make this department a profit center. I think I'll be pushed out if I don't leave of my own accord. Is it worth sticking around to collect the severance pay I have coming?"

Finding a new job when you're close to or over fifty can be tough, as Beth knew from Lawry's experience. But a "job" may not be what you want when you've reached the peak of your career. You may be able to earn a good living while enjoying far more autonomy as an independent contractor or consultant. Severance pay and continuing fringe benefits may be exactly what you need to start something new, perhaps do the thing you've always dreamed of doing.

Beth saw all the warning signs in her insurance company and mapped out a plan to join one of her vendors in a firm that provided training programs for large companies. After thinking it over, she waited to be given her notice and collected severance pay. "More money than I'd ever expected! Enough for a cushion while I took the risk of partnership with a vendor," she said. "Not waiting for that money would have only been an ego trip." Even in her new partnership, however, Beth's worries weren't over.

Many have a hard time reaching a happy landing after bailing out. **You may know the "color of your parachute," but find it battered and buffeted by what you're experiencing!** The financial settlement may be less generous than you anticipated. You may not have access to your former office and secretary as Lawry did during outplacement. New opportunities may be scarce, especially for those at the peak of their careers.

It's far easier to market yourself to a new employer if you take the initiative before being "pink-slipped." Employers like to think they're hiring you away from another company, not bringing you in out of the cold. You may also perceive yourself differently if you're job hunting before being forced out. As Elinor discovered, "Getting fired is the pits! Even if it's not your fault. Even if it's happening to everybody. It took me a long time to build my self-esteem to the point where I could 'sell' a new employer on my abilities."

If you're job hunting while still working at your old job, emphasize the need for confidentiality in any correspondence. Before leaving an interview, ask if the person has any reservations about your qualifications so you can address them right on the spot.

If being terminated is inevitable and you have an opportunity for outplacement counseling, by all means take advantage of it for the objective feedback and job-marketing advice you'll get. Once you're job hunting after being laid off, show a positive attitude about your future and avoid going on interviews until you can project such an attitude. Focus instead on the opportunity you're seeking. Don't discuss personalities or seem to be negative. Emphasize what you can do for the new company.

With a little preparation, you may be able to act in time to avoid the trauma of being let go. Meanwhile, get your résumé in shape and activate Plan B. If you ride the wave until wipe-out as Beth did, make sure it's a conscious choice you've made after considering all the options.

Moving On

Ten percent of us change jobs in a given year, and ten percent will change careers in the next five years. Obsolete skills will force one third of current workers to shift during this time, according to the Bureau of Labor Statistics.

Most of the women in my research left their jobs to get away from bad situations or the stress of working hard without seeing payoffs for themselves. A whopping fifty percent said they'd been briefly plateaued at one time in their careers, for such reasons as bosses, discrimination and lack of tenure. Thirty percent moved on to escape boredom and burnout.

One woman who was typical said, "I gave it my best. But I wasn't moving along as I'd hoped. I saw younger, less qualified men zoom out from behind again and again. I was still expected to put in a sixty-hour week and adapt my schedule to fit the company's needs. I wanted to go where I'd be appreciated, where I could see some results from the effort I put forth."

Research continues to show that many women leave one company for another because they haven't found the opportunities and challenges they'd hoped for. You're far from alone if you're convinced that no women will be promoted beyond a certain level in your company and you want to go further. Allison was in this position earlier when she realized she'd never be corporate secretary. Maybe there's no child-care program and you'd rather work where there is one. These are valid reasons for leaving, but will you find what you're looking for elsewhere?

In *The Best Companies for Women*, Baila Zeitz and Lorraine Dusky examined corporate policies, statistics and benefits in the recruiting, hiring and promoting of women; the actual numbers of women in upper levels; sex discrimination and harassment, flexibility regarding pregnancy and parenting. No companies were perfect, they found. Informed choices and flexibility are the watchwords because every company is different, as their investigation of fifty-two of the best shows.

How can you tell if a new situation is a good choice? Put *all* your coping skills into play in reaching a decision. A Leaper might follow her instincts, overlooking some important factors. Elinor liked the image projected by a certain store, but she never guessed the company would be bought out. A more seasoned Leaper would use a strategic focus on future possibilities.

Some Listeners accept jobs where they like the people, ignoring other important factors. They think things will work out because the atmosphere "feels right." Mature Listener skills enable you to see where you'd function as an effective member of a team.

A Lister would write down the job factors she considers important. Perhaps she wants to manage a large budget and staff for her department, and to have a chance for a raise in six months. She might steer clear of chaotic environments, in favor of those where she's more in control. She also has a salary range she expects. Among fringe benefits she wants health insurance and a range of options from which to choose. As she looks into job opportunities, she keeps track of which companies offer the items on her list. As she gets closer to being hired, she negotiates for items she wants that the company considers optional.

A Logical might begin with a similar list of items to satisfy, but would also look at the "what ifs." She'd be prepared for trade-offs. She'd figure the dollar value of fringe benefits and of time spent commuting.

A Learner incorporates all of these skills in weighing her options. Not only that, she considers the job search itself a chance to learn more about industries, companies, people and arenas in which she can test her abilities.

Rather than zigzagging to similar companies, many women in large companies prefer switching to smaller ones. This isn't necessarily a step down. In a smaller company, you may have a greater range of responsibilities, and a chance to learn other functions besides your own. You can play a more important role in reaching the company goals. One South Carolina study found almost fifty-one percent of women employed by large firms were unmarried, while only thirty-four percent employed by smaller companies were unmarried. Although they worked for the same reasons as other women, the study found those in small companies seemed to have less need for power over others. Perhaps the smaller companies were more flexible or attracted women with different ambitions.

As she considered leaving her large cosmetics company, Diana looked into a job with a small communications vendor. "My pros for the move include more influence in decisions, potentially more money through their bonus system and a chance to learn marketing. I'm concerned about the 'fit' with two new partners there, but I think it will work. I'll miss my old friends and I know I'll have to work long hours at first. The new office is pretty shabby too, but that's a minor element. I can fix it up."

As you contemplate a move, also consider what shape your overall career may be taking. If you're out of work, you might fall back on a Contingency Career for income during your job search. If you already have a Concurrent Career that generates earnings, you'll have an added cushion to see you through a transition. If you don't have one of the alternate career patterns in place before becoming unemployed, you're probably best off focusing on your "main" career now.

However, possibilities you'd never dreamed of may present themselves. For example, you're an engineer but you hear of an opportunity marketing technical equipment. Or you're a sportswear buyer but someone offers you a chance to organize a trade show. Before saying no to something far-fetched, temporary or part-time, consider how it will affect your long-range ambitions. Ask yourself too if it helps you build competencies, adds to your experience, contacts, marketability or future income.

Having Combination Careers involves being open to very different things, but may serve you well. Leapers and Learners who welcome a chance to leave the beaten path aren't the only ones who stand to benefit. The drawback, as noted earlier, is the difficulty in describing what you've done on your résumé. Pinpoint the transferable skills and competencies you've acquired within the description of your accomplishments.

BECOMING AN INDEPENDENT

Why not join the sweeping movement away from corporate careers toward self-employment? A *Fortune* magazine study of M.B.A.'s from seventeen prestigious business schools found that sixty-nine percent of *both* men and women initially chose large corporations or professional firms, but that ten years later, thirty percent of the women and twenty-one percent of the men were self-employed, unemployed or listed no occupation. A recent survey of *Wall Street Journal* readers earning $100,000 or more showed seventy-five percent would choose a different profession if they could start over again and seventy-one percent would rather be self-employed!

For some, becoming independent means going for it in a big way, risking your own and other people's money in hopes of making a killing in a few years. Perhaps you have an idea with multimillion-dollar potential that could lure venture capitalists. Perhaps you've been told you'd make a good entrepreneur.

Not everybody is cut out for it. **To grow a business takes tremendous drive, ambition, long hours and personal sacrifice.** Leapers are more likely to start businesses, often as not "leaping in" without considering the downside. Those who succeed, however, have tempered their Leaper competencies with a strong dose of Lister skills as well as Logical and Listener ones. They are already Learners or they become so, or they find people for their team who complement their skills and expertise.

Savvy Woman annually lists sixty top women business owners. Their cutoff was $39 million and above in sales for 1990, with the top two over a billion dollars each. They're still very rare at this level, but if your dream is to join them, look for quizzes, books, seminars and advisers to help you assess your chances. Plan to put in years of work to make it happen.

Many others with less capacity for risk or round-the-clock work and with little or no money nevertheless find they are well suited to working independently, outside the corporate world. If you're one of these, you might call yourself a consultant, a vendor, a free-lancer.

Leapers, with their dislike for authority, yearn to cut themselves loose from their employers, but individuals from the other styles may make this adjustment easily too. Women especially like the autonomy, whether their ultimate goals are high earnings or more time with families. Because businesses can save money by hiring independents, the trend is spreading rapidly, along with agencies that match people and companies.

An increasing number of women professionals work as consultants while building reputations around their core expertise. They work in training, communications and technical fields. Some earn high fees. As independent contractors, they receive no benefits, so they must pay their own insurance and expenses though they enjoy the same tax benefits as small businesses.

For all practical purposes, they *are* in business for themselves, never knowing what tomorrow may bring. One woman, who'd been derailed from a Classic Career, comments, "There could be lean times ahead, but almost nothing could wipe me out the way being fired once did. I consider this more secure than most jobs."

Some must market their services aggressively. Others, especially in technical professions, work through agencies that do their marketing for a fee. One woman built her computer/management information systems skills with three such assignments before joining a major corporation again at a higher level.

Some women increase their odds for success by taking on one or more partners. Good partners can be friends or colleagues with complementary skills—financial or marketing, for example. A partner doesn't have to be an intimate friend, but should be somebody you trust, enjoy being with and with whom you can easily be candid. It's also important for you to share the same vision for your enterprise and agree on ethical standards and ways of operating.

One woman had three women partners to help her swing the investment in a travel-related business. "Never again," she said. "I'd rather go it alone!" And she did, in a second new business, with employees who didn't challenge her decisions and "silent-partner" help from her brother with a loan. Often friends or family come to the rescue with funds to get started, because getting loans from banks is tough without a track record. Divorce settlements have launched some women's businesses. If a second mortgage on your house or condo is the only source of seed money, you should think carefully before risking the roof over your head.

Your best partner may actually turn out to be your spouse. More and more couples are going into business together—over 480,000 in a five-year period. Eleven of the fifty fastest-growing franchise chains listed by *Venture* magazine were founded by couples. In many businesses the woman is the more visible member of the team as Liz Claiborne and Debbi Fields were in the eighties. When they're good, family businesses can be very good, but they can also strain relationships to the breaking point and beyond.

Independent ventures fit with each of the different career shapes. Beth was doing it in a Concentric way with her teaching and writing, building on her core of technical training expertise. Diana, open to a variety of ways of putting her skills to use, was hoping for a Combination Career as an independent writer and communications expert.

There are some disadvantages besides not having fringe benefits. As Diana knew, you're an outsider and not part of a regular team or social circle at work. You have to make up for the lack of structure by being self-motivated and highly disciplined. Your status could drop. It's up to you to give yourself the image you want with your business cards, address and answering service as well as with your client list. There may be less income too. Free-lance fees look higher until you consider the expenses plus the time it takes for the marketing and administrative work that doesn't pay.

Women with family responsibilities may willingly accept the downside in order to spend more time at home. Those who can negotiate a part-time link with their existing employer, as Allison did after the birth of her son, may have an easier time than "independents." Allison knew which days she'd be in the office and how large her paycheck would be. She was left juggling phone calls, scheduling appointments around naps and closing off space for her "office" at home. The woman with an independent business has as many practical worries plus uncertainty about earnings and when clients will expect her to jump.

Although Diana knew the disadvantages after working from home when her children were infants, she wanted to do it again. "Sure, it's hard. Sure, I'd miss my office friends. But this is what I want. This is what makes me feel the most creative, the most free. I'll have to wait until we can afford the financial risk, but I know I'll be happy." "Happy" is a word others use, along with "autonomous" and "free." But Diana was wise to heed the financial warnings.

Being an independent isn't something many consultants and free-lancers planned far in advance. Some turned full-time jobs into part-time work. Others were out of work and accepted a temporary assignment, then one thing led to another and their businesses grew.

There are also those who go back to traditional employment, some seeing themselves as better off for the varied experiences they've had and others regretting time "lost."

Working for yourself can put your life in sync with your changing definition of success—a sense of achievement, a balanced life, personal satisfaction or service to others and financial rewards.

A New Location

Life-style issues loom larger for virtually everyone these days. **Where people live may be even more important than what they do.** In numbers that would have seemed incredible just a few years ago, women, and increasingly men too, are trading earning power for a better quality of life.

Many people don't want to relocate or even look for work elsewhere. They may be kept by family ties, lower costs of living, specialized skills not needed elsewhere and often simply because they like the life-style. Fifty percent of Stanford University's potentially mobile class of 1988 chose to stay in California. Southerners, New Englanders and Texans may be content to stay where they are too.

But perhaps you want to start fresh in a new setting. Even after looking at ways to change your balance of activities and your life-style where you are, you still crave a different environment.

This type of move involves many considerations. Look closely at your reasons for leaving where you are now. **Will the "baggage" you take with you include the very things you're hoping to escape? Does the new location offer sufficient opportunities for employment, social life, intellectual stimulation and spare-time activities? Are there people, places and intangible things you'd miss more than you realize? Look for signs that the economy is healthy with potential growth in your field.**

For decades, large cities have been magnets for achievement-oriented people. Up-and-coming Classic Careerists would gravitate toward the hub of their industries, drawn by the promise of advancement. Many professional women like the quickened pace and the numerous amenities. Beth went to New York for the job opportunities, the cultural advantages and the privacy, no small consideration at the time. Other women have forsaken small towns and family ties to be where no one knows about a divorce or a scandal they wanted to forget. Some suburban empty-nesters move back to the city, drawn by entertainment, shopping, medical facilities and overall convenience.

Meanwhile, many city dwellers today long for a saner and safer, if slower, existence away from the major metropolitan centers. One single mother moved her family from a large city in the Northeast to medium-sized Portland, Oregon. The pluses were proximity to her parents, the friendly life-style, good schools and the outdoor sports. Although she doesn't take home as much money as before, her rent and everyday expenses are lower too. Another unmarried woman chose a country home close enough for commuting to her city job. The trees, the fresh air and the sense of putting down roots in a stable community are some of the reasons why.

Not everyone joining the exodus is pleased with the greener pastures, however. A woman from Los Angeles settled in a smaller town up the coast to avoid the smog, the frantic freeway travel and the stress while taking advantage of a difference in housing costs. "I have a view of the ocean I couldn't have afforded before. But I miss the people and the activities in the city. If I had it to do over, I wouldn't leave," she says.

If you want to move, yet don't know where, let your fingers do the walking initially. Rand McNally rates places to live by climate, housing, cost of living, quality of life and other factors in *Places Rated Almanac, Vacation Places Rated* and *Retirement Places Rated*, and gives facts and figures for every town of over a hundred people in *Randata City Index*. Travel sections in your bookstore, libraries, geographical indexes of industries and companies, local yellow pages, Chambers of Commerce and state tourist offices are helpful too.

What's the best city for you? *Savvy Woman* rates the best and worst cities for women. Consider Seattle, Pittsburgh, Minneapolis–St. Paul, Atlanta and others. Baltimore, St. Louis and San Antonio have had their make-overs too. The Research Triangle in North Carolina, San Diego, the Southwest—Phoenix, Albuquerque, Santa Fe—may suit you. By all means try visiting first.

The business press will give you a sense of where the growing markets are. Your own priorities, however, may include nearness to family or kindred spirits, universities, your favorite sports activities or the climate that agrees with you best. And no matter how adventuresome you are, you probably won't be happy for long without people with whom you have things in common, such as single status or similar values.

SOCIAL ENTREPRENEURING

Social entrepreneuring for an idea, cause or social concern can be a stepping-stone in your career, or, for those with independent means or in their retirement years, it can be the culmination of all you've done until now, the supreme challenge of your life.

There's no shortage of areas in which professionals can ply their talents. Lawyers are moving into advocacy roles for the homeless, AIDS patients, welfare recipients and numerous environmental issues. Individuals sponsor underprivileged students with the promise of college if they graduate from high school. People are setting up nonprofit associations for the development of affordable housing. Women have traditionally done much of the work in not-for-profits, but men are becoming more involved now too.

Many women expect nonprofit organizations will be more democratic and egalitarian and less rigid than profit-making enterprises. They're often disappointed. Many of the nonprofits, especially the well-established ones, are no less bureaucratic, political and turf-minded, and can be more so. The maneuvering to get on prestigious boards can be ruthless. One woman who'd spent most of her career working for health-related nonprofits finally left for the private sector. "I thought profit was not the right way to motivate employees, but when people are watching the bottom line, at least everybody agrees on that goal and you know where they're coming from. With people who aren't out to make money, you can only guess at what's motivating them." If you're looking for an organization that reflects all your values, you may have to start your own, as many women have.

Government service is another way to give back socially. The cliché that people go to Washington to do good and leave to do well seems to be true for men more than for women. When trying to place high-level women from the Carter administration, we at Catalyst found the response of business shockingly discouraging. Although the women had managed multimillion-dollar budgets and staffs in the hundreds, businesses had almost no comparable openings for them.

As I said starting out, you have opportunities for new beginnings at *any* age. Remember, no matter what your stage in life, times of crisis and change may lie ahead. The key is to be flexible and willing to learn, always adding to your stockpile of skills, competencies and resources. Whatever your choice, remember the motto *Have assets, will travel.*

You may not yet know the answer to the question "What's next in your life?" but I hope you'll frame the question in a positive, productive way. Instead of asking "What am I going to do now?" ask "Which of the many interesting things that I could do will I choose next?" The exercise that follows and those in the final chapter will help you sort it out.

EXERCISE II

WHERE ARE YOU NOW?

1. Imagine that you've encountered a long-lost friend, someone who was once your bosom buddy. It could be a man or a woman, but this is someone you trust and are happy to see.

You schedule an evening together to get caught up. What would you say has happened to you in the past decade or two? Jot down the major events.

"Since the last time I saw you . . . _____

_____

_____

_____

_____

_____has happened."

2. "My God!" she or he says. "How did you *cope* with all of that?

"Well, I just . . . _____

_____

_____

_____

and then I . . . _____

_____

All in all, _____, _____, _____

_____, _____

__ _____

were my most helpful resources," you say, commenting on your health as you talk.

3. "Did you find yourself changed by the years? What did you learn about yourself?" she or he next asks.

"I learned I have a particular way of approaching problems. I use styles I

call _____

_____

which means I usually prefer to _____

when faced with a dilemma. But I've altered my way of coping with conflicts." I now cope by _____

_____

_____

_____

4. "Do you think we've been shaped by our times?" she or he then asks.

"Oh, yes, I've realized _____

_____

_____

trends have affected me. How about you?" (It's your turn to listen.)

5. "What a fabulous evening," she or he says, hugging you good night. You leave on a high with promises to stay in touch *this* time.

As you relax in the shower later, other thoughts bubble up: things you wished you had told him or her about your relationships, life-style or anything else. Jot them down while they're fresh. _____

_____

_____

You may have seen new patterns or gained new insights from your talk. What are they? _____

_____

_____

These questions are designed to help clarify what you've learned about yourself up to now. As you take a life-span perspective, look at *all* the elements that are or will be important to your sense of well-being, now and in the coming years.

As with our five women friends, you've surely added new ways of coping, new strategies and resources.

PROGRESS REPORT

Here we've explored a variety of options for those who anticipate or dream of changes.

The five women were also in the midst of career moves.

Elinor was planning for her own business, building on her retailing background. She was lining up backers, potential partners, locations and sources of supply before she moves. Although still in her associate buyer's job, she was doing double duty in her travels, making contacts, having samples made, testing them on weekends.

"I'd have leapt right into this before," she admitted, "but it's smarter to proceed cautiously and get advice from experts. There's stuff I just don't know, especially financial." She was keeping careful records of her flea-market business until time to make her move, and was paying off her debts. The former accountant from her family's pharmacy, a gentleman near seventy and a great fan of Elinor's, provided practical help.

Diana, after much weighing of pros and cons and discussions with Nate, joined one of her communications vendors. "It's a step toward the independent consulting and writing life I really want," she said. "Nate and I decided we couldn't risk that financially yet.

"I'm learning more about annual-report production, which is a good field to know. I hire free-lancers a lot, so I can see what others offer." She apologized for the smallness of her new office, but, as she promised, she'd decorated it with bright Mexican serapes and some of her own artwork on the walls. "It's interesting working for a company with only forty people. I'll soon know everybody!"

Responding to market conditions, Carole decided to put real estate on the back burner for the present. "It's a shame because good people are needed to make housing affordable," she said. "I'll come back to it in a few years." She interviewed for several jobs and kept in touch with two executive search firms, then the opportunity she'd dreamed of came along. "I'm going to work in Paris! They liked my marketing background with smart cards and my willingness to work abroad. With the European Economic Community and the changes in Eastern Europe, this is the most exciting place to be." She'll be in financial services with the European branches of her new company, which is testing similar cards in every country. "I'm taking crash courses in French and I leave in two weeks! Ro is helping me find an apartment not far from hers, and she has a man she wants me to meet." Opportunity appeared and Carole grabbed it.

Even after careful planning, Beth hadn't been so fortunate in her career move. After her outplacement she formed a partnership with a male colleague. Unfortunately, he wasn't accustomed to sharing ideas or listening to anyone else's, even Beth's input. "It was a big disappointment. Then Lawry had a bypass operation and my old arthritis kicked up. But the good news is that last summer we got married after all this time! So, you see, I'm learning to take risks after all." She fairly glowed.

"Also, Lawry and I have formed a business partnership," she added. "He has his clients and I have mine. My old company is one of my clients and I've added others from my network."

Allison decided to leave her company after Scott entered a college where alternating paid work and study in a co-op program will help support him. True to form, Allison was looking further down the road than the others. She mentioned that Keith planned to take early retirement the next time it was offered. His severance package would help carry him until his pension kicked in and included continued health coverage and seminars on starting a business. "We're already minor equity partners with two friends in an environmental consulting firm. We work evenings and weekends. No one knows it at work and they won't until I'm ready." She added, "It *feels* good, making this change. *Feels!* I never thought I'd use that word!"

Each of the five altered her ambitions with changes in her major life areas: career, relationships, self-development, health and life-style. Each approached the challenges differently, gradually going beyond her main coping style to use a broader mix of resources and strategies. Finally, each had learned enough to create a life more in balance with her needs.

As I've been promising you all along, you too can shape your life to get more of the things you want. In the final chapter, we'll get down to business, drafting your five-year plan and plotting the time lines to keep it on schedule. Although there'll be unexpected challenges ahead, with planning, you can make each new wrinkle fit into the overall pattern you want for your life.

CHAPTER IX

Putting It All Together

WHETHER you look at your future as a challenge, an adventure, a chance to learn or a series of choices, it's time to put together the different elements that you've learned and repackage your life to make it more viable for the future. You'll be writing much of this chapter yourself, by completing exercises where you'll make choices and draw up workable plans for what's next in your life. I'll still be here as your coach, of course, and the five women who've been our models will provide some concrete examples.

Here's how they described what they've learned.

Allison offered: "Putting it all together to me means combining the best from my past with what I've learned about expanding my coping abilities. Yes, the old New England values of saving and working hard are still with me, but struggling with the difficulties in our family—our son's drug problem and my father's illness—I've learning to trust my feelings more. I used to think emotions had nothing to do with earning a living. Well, now I'm making a career change and my gut-level feelings are a big part of my motivation. That and my conscience. Of course, I'm checking out all the angles and proceeding with caution."

In spite of the failure of her first business partnership, Beth looked more relaxed than the last few times I'd seen her. "Yes, I've learned I can live without being in control of everything. Just that realization helped me decide to risk being a bride at fifty-two. I know I can't 'fix' Lawry or make him over to be perfect. The only person I can change is me, and once again, I'm remaking my life."

Carole was "putting her act together" in new ways. "I've always got an audience—young minorities behind me. I have to set a good example. But I'm proud of what I've accomplished so far, and my parents would be too. Now I've taken on a bigger challenge—making a career in Europe and finding a suitable mate, if I can. If I can't, I'm pretty sure I can live with just me. Meanwhile, I learn something every day just being in a new country. For example, I approach social problems differently. Who knows what opportunities lie ahead? Now the curtain's rising on Act Two!"

Diana laughed her characteristically warm laugh. "Putting it all together is like bringing all your talents and insights to a novel or a painting. I have an idea in my mind, but amazing things happen and it all changes. I have no problem being open to new things, but I've learned that I need to be more disciplined and structured. That goes for my creative work as well as my career. As time goes on too, my career really is my creative work. The inner me and the outer me aren't in conflict as they once were. I used to fight 'distractions' in order to retreat deep within. But with a more structured life, I have a little bit of solitude every day as well as time with people. And I love it all. I'd never have imagined I could love my life as much as I do. I learned how after I thought I was losing it!"

"Putting my life together is like dressing in the morning or packing for a trip," Elinor bubbled. "I have a certain look that I want. I know the sum total of that look but there are infinite ways of achieving it. I used to just grab this and that, you know, rely on trial and error until something worked. I still experiment! I do super-original things! But I have a better idea of what doesn't work so I have fewer failures. Fewer failures in my wardrobe and in what I sell! Am I becoming a logical person? Or just a better gambler? I want it to be fun along the way, know what I mean?" I do.

So patience, Leapers and others too. This final push will help you clarify your future ambitions in light of what's going to work for you.

EXERCISE I

IMAGINING WHAT'S NEXT

1. You've already written down some thoughts about your future. But circumstances may demand more than one plan. To be safe, you need several

scenarios: Plans A, B and C to move you in the direction you want to go, even if you take a zigzag path. Let's see what they'd be.

Rather than filling in blanks, Leapers and Learners and others too may prefer doing a mind map. You'll need some large sheets of blank paper and crayons or colored pencils. Write Plan A in the center as you did with your Relationships Constellation. Instead of drawing circles, now try branching out as if with the limbs of a tree as you think about each aspect of your plan.

For example, the career section could include one branch each for boss, compensation, responsibilities, and so on, with smaller branches that describe the characteristics you'd like in each element, such as friendly, equity, manage a division. One woman put a heart at the center as a symbol for her plan. Her branches looked like arteries spread out in all directions. Do a mind map for each of the three plans if you prefer. Note the patterns each makes.

Plan A

2. You're at lunch with a friend five years from now in a setting in which you can speak undisturbed for a while. This could be the same or a different friend from the one you used in the previous exercise.

Again imagine that this friend hasn't seen you for the last five years and is all ears to catch up with you. Imagine what ideally would have happened in those five years.

"What's happened?" he or she asks and you begin.

"Well, my career is _____

_____

_____.

"And I'm living (with, in) _____

_____.

_____.

"I spend my free time _____

_____.

"The news about my family is _____

_____.

"To keep my mind and body challenged, I'm _____

_____.

"My health is ———————————————————.

"That sounds great!" your friend says. "It's good to see you so happy, looking so good." You feel the same about her/him.

PLAN B

3. Now imagine that, instead of Plan A, Plan B has come true instead.

You're spending a weekend at a spa five years from now. Everyone is relaxed and you're sharing your story with a few good friends who haven't seen you in all this time.

"It's funny how things turn out. My career is ———————————

—————————————————————————

—————————————————————————.

"I'm living (in, with) ————————————————————

—————————————————————————

—————————————————————————.

"I love spending my free time ——————————————————

—————————————————————————.

In fact I've recently ——————————————————————

—————————————————————————.

"My health is ———————————————————————

—————————————————————————.

"My family's ——————————————————————

—————————————————————————.

"As usual, you're amazing," say your friends. "You just keep getting better."

PLAN C

4. On a Concorde to London, five years from now, you run into a friend you haven't seen in five years. The last time you talked, you told your friend about Plan B. Things haven't worked out as you'd expected, but you're pleased with where you are and what's happened.

"Bring me up to date on your life," your companion says, after you've arranged to be seated together.

You say, "Well, instead of _____

_____,

I'm now _____

_____

in my career."

"My life-style, as you may have guessed, _____

_____

and I'm living (with, in) _____

_____.

"My family _____

_____.

"When I have a free moment, I _____

_____.

Lately I've _____

_____

for my health."

"It's been an interesting five years," notes your friend. "Let's see some theater together this trip. I want to hear more." You're delighted to have the company and arrange to meet later that week.

Of course, you could have Plans D and E too, but let's start with these three.

5. These additional career exercises will give you an even longer-term perspective on your future.

A. Imagine you've just won a $10 million lottery. How would your Plans A, B and C differ? What else would you do with the windfall? What provisions would you make for other people?

_____

_____

_____

_____

Even if you don't get the windfall, you may be able to accomplish some of your dreams with less money.

B. It's the evening of your retirement dinner, where your professional colleagues, business and personal friends and family have gathered to honor you. What are they saying about what you've accomplished in your career?

What are the highlights and peak moments of your career? _____

_____

_____

_____

_____

They sing "Thanks for the Memories" with words from *your* life.

What else do these questions suggest that you'd like to achieve? Any new ambitions? What paths not taken from your past would you like to reconsider now? (If you need a reminder, take a look at what you've said in the exercises throughout the book.) The point is to cover all your bases in shaping your plan.

6. In making your plans, setting your goals and achieving them, think of yourself as CEO of your own assets, chair of the board of your Altered Ambitions Committee.

For this purpose, assemble an Advisory Board Constellation of individuals you want for advice and emotional support, those who bring competencies and expertise you don't have. Who would you want around your table?

YOUR BOARD MEMBERS

Logicals	_____	_____	_____
Listers	_____	_____	_____
Listeners	_____	_____	_____
Leapers	_____	_____	_____
Learners	_____	_____	_____

If you're planning to start a business, think of experts in the functions you'll need—financial (Logicals), managerial (Listers), human resources (Listeners), strategic and creative (Leapers and Learners)—and people who've built businesses themselves. That's covering all the bases with your Board.

Imagine too what Allison, Beth, Carole, Diana and Elinor would say about your plans.

"Have you considered your alternatives? Weighed your options? Prioritized them?" Allison asks.

"What steps do you need to take to get from here to there? Have you checked this out in the 'real' world? Is it practical?" Beth admonishes.

"What will you learn from each opportunity? Where will it take you toward your goals? Does it build on your strengths?" Carole questions.

"What are the people like? Is the chemistry good? Does it feel like a fit?" Diana wonders.

"Will you have any fun or does it look like another grind? Where's the adventure? Does it energize you? Then go for it!" Elinor enthuses.

These are the kinds of differing perspectives you'll want.

This series of exercises is designed to help you tap into the many dreams and ideas you may have for the future. Although you may have to eliminate a few, at least you're now more aware of what you want. To make these dreams reality, you now have to act.

Let's plan for your actions in Exercise II. You could do it *without* having done all the other exercises, but you'd be missing many pieces, handicapping yourself unnecessarily and perhaps repeating old patterns that are no longer effective. If you complete the *whole* process, your results will be much richer, reflecting many different facets of who you are.

EXERCISE II

GOING FOR YOUR GOAL
YOUR FINAL PLAN A

Realistically, now, which pieces of your Plans A, B and C are most doable for now? Which pieces lead strategically to where you'd *really* like to be in your life five years from now? Although you could pull from each to make new synergistic Plans A, B and C, let's concentrate on whatever you decide is Plan A for you now.

Once you've been through the process with A, you can always use B or C as fallbacks, if you need to.

Describe it in as much detail as you can:

1. **Your preferred field,** specialty and function: _____

_____

_____

2. Your preferred **industries** or **arenas** in which to work, sectors of the
economy: _____

_____

_____

3. Your preferred **types of employers,** if you want a Classic Career or your
preferred **customers** or **clients** if you want to start a business: (List
specific companies or organizations.) _____

_____

_____

_____

4. Your preferred **Career Shape** if not Classic up-the-ladder in a large or
medium-sized organization is:

◎ **Concentric**—Building on a core, as in a business or product
line. _____

▤ **Concurrent**—Having two or more parallel, major activities in
tandem. _____

☺ **Combination**—Having a variety of unrelated activities, including

_____

▭▭▭ **Contingency**—Doing something you love that may not pay well on a
regular basis, and having a fallback activity to earn money. _____

Your choice for now is a _____ career shape.
You may want to try _____ in the future.

5. Your preferred **responsibilities** (What's a typical day like? What skills
are you using?): _____

_____

_____

6. Your preferred **title(s)** and **compensation** (salary, equity, benefits, bonus, perks, and so on): _____

_____

_____

7. Where are your **multiple streams of income** going to come from? ____

_____

_____

8. What is your preferred **work environment** (desk job, on the run, travel, telecommute, part-time, flexitime, full-time, a mix of these?) and preferred **organization culture** (hard driving, laid back, friendly, competitive, etc.)? _____

_____

9. What's your preferred type of **boss** (mentor, delegator, powerful and so on) **or partner**? What personality characteristics does this person have?

_____

_____

_____

10. Your preferred **life-style** (geographical location, living quarters, living arrangements): _____

_____

11. Your preferred **relationships** (including changes to make): _____

_____

_____

_____

12. Your preferred **mental** and **physical** states (including changes to make about your health or stress levels): _____

_____

13. What **trends** might affect your plans? _____

_____

_____

_____

14. What additional **competencies** do you need? (As you noted in Exercise I, Chapter VII)? _____

_____

_____

15. What other **contacts, experiences and education** do you need as **stepping-stones** to achieving your five-year plan? _____

_____

_____

_____

Although you won't be able to get everything you want, you'll come closer if you have **a framework and some guidelines** to help you focus your search and assess offers or opportunities that arise. As they come along, ask Do I really want this? Do I want it enough to make the trade-offs and sacrifices necessary? Will I continue to learn or is this more of the same? Does it move me toward the goals I have for my life (even if my goal is to cut back or retire)?

Now envision yourself there. What's a typical day like? Do you need any further adjustments to what you see? Do you like the person you've become?

As you shape your life and career toward your *own* vision, you're limited only by that vision, the effort you put forth and the resources you draw on to achieve it.

Now you're ready to start making it happen.

YOUR ACTION PLAN

Use whatever calendar, tickler file or planning guide works best for you in looking at time lines for the pieces of your plan. Here are some suggestions for a job campaign, but reorder and adapt them to suit yourself and the type of changes you've been making.

1. *Month #1*
   Preparation for Your Job Campaign
   • **Get an advisory board in place.** Line up people you can call on as needed though not in a formalized way. Let them

react to and refine your plans and résumé. Get their help in sticking to a timetable if you need it. Assure them that you'll do the same for them.

- **Update your résumé.** In its new version it will serve as a marketing tool. Write your professional objective and skills summary at the top of the résumé, with the details filled in below. Focus on your accomplishments beyond mere duties and responsibilities. Combine chronological with functional sections if that "positions" you more effectively. Highlight achievements and competencies with bullets. Quantify your achievements with impressive numbers. (Even if you plan to stay with your present employer, the process is sound contingency planning. It can also be useful for internal promotional interviews.) Reproduce it on quality bond paper with matching letterhead for the cover letter and envelope.
- **Put your contact list in order**—colleagues, vendors, past associates, your network, Rolodex, directories, and so on.
- **Prioritize the list into** (A) those who might have a job or some business for you, (B) those who probably can't hire you, but can refer you to others, and (C) those who can give you information on opportunities or who can contribute ideas for your campaign.
- **Rehearse your pitch** (whether for your current employer, your own business or a job search). Answer questions about your accomplishments, strengths, one weakness framed as a strength, why you should be hired, what your goals are. Do live role playing with someone who can critique your presentation. (See the career books at the end of the book for more help if you need it.)

Campaign Action
- **Launch your campaign** for a promotion, new responsibility or next move. **Remember, it will take time.**
- **Make daily and weekly "to-do" lists** with names to call, letters to write and ads to answer. Try to get two or three referrals from each contact so your lists keep expanding. Thank *everyone* who helps or tries to. Keep your network alive and growing.
- **Go on interviews, stay visible, spend twenty-five to forty**

hours a week on your job search efforts even if it's evenings and weekends. That's what your competition is doing.

2. *Months #2 to 6*
   - **Keep at the process.** Revise your goals as the situation changes, including goals for relationships, health, continued learning.
   - **Consider Plans B and C,** if A is not working.
   - **Strategize with your Board.** Don't try to go it alone.
   - **Keep your energy and positive attitude going.** Look at how far you've come.

3. *Month #?*
   - **Goal attained.** Celebrate. Thank everyone you've contacted in your search and let them know where you've landed. Be ready to do them favors too.
   - **Set your next stepping-stone goals.** Good luck.

You can follow similar campaigns and steps to improve your relationships, health, and life-style, too. But, as you can see, this is a lot of work. Millions make major changes every year, but they don't make them so thoroughly, and many make more mistakes and are far less satisfied with the results than you'll be. With your new learning and competencies, you should be ready for *whatever* happens next and what you want to happen.

Before you ride off into the sunset, let's take a final look at Allison, Beth, Carole, Diana and Elinor. They're further along now. They've reached more of their goals, made some major changes and have broader life perspectives, as you will too.

CODA—FINAL PROGRESS REPORT

ALLISON'S NEW CHALLENGES

I visited Allison at her Teaneck house, which I scarcely recognized. She and Keith had renovated it. On one side was a home office with two desks, two computers, conference table and plenty of filing cabinets.

Allison wore the jacket to one of her older power suits over a T-shirt and slacks. Her sleeves were rolled up. The image combined the "new" and the "old" Allison attractively.

"This is where I'll be working very soon. I can hardly wait. I got my spurt of action when we had that last oil spill." She explained that she'd gone to the area to help her company's local attorneys handle claims filed against the company for the damage to the coast. "It's the birds and animals that suffer," she said sadly. "And people will eventually suffer too. That's why I'm going over to the other side. Lawyers are needed to help draft legislation and to represent other interests here."

As planned, Keith had taken early retirement after his company made him an offer too good to refuse. Having taken biochemistry courses for two years before retirement, he'd been ready to make the transition to environmental consulting. "He's at different sites every day," said Allison. "He loves it. I will too. It's great not having to answer to different bosses and making our own hours. The only danger is we tend to work all the time, which is one reason we've compartmentalized our house like this. We need time and space just for us."

She explained that both Kathy and Scott were away at school. Kathy was starting pre-med at Yale, and Scott was hoping to combine computer graphics and business interests. "He *seems* off to a promising start. We're with him every step of the way—but at a respectable distance."

I asked her when she'd be making the move from her Classic Career at the oil company into the new venture with her husband. "Well, they're moving their headquarters to New Orleans later this year, and I'm *not* going with them," she said. "Once Keith and I close one more contract, there'll be no financial problem in resigning. We have backup funds in case of an emergency, but don't want to dip into them unless we have to. I'm so glad we did all that advance preparation. We're finally doing work we believe in and are getting paid for it too. My dad would have been proud." Her expression darkened, but only momentarily. I didn't ask about her father's status, but I sensed that whatever it was, she had come to terms with it and cherished her memories of him. Said Allison, "I've never felt so alive!" She had found a cause that had altered her ambitions and life-style again.

BETH'S ONGOING CHOICES

Beth and Lawry had become partners in their growing Management Information Systems and computer-training business. Their clients were small to medium-sized companies trying to expand office automation.

They worked with a number of suppliers too, and got commissions on additional sales they and their three employees made. "We're doing pretty well," said Beth after ushering me into their new apartment.

After selling their East Side co-op at a profit, they moved to a charmingly renovated building near Union Square. They had a second bedroom that they used as a guest room and office. "This keeps our overhead down. It's big enough for now, since our employees don't spend much time here."

Beth's hair was grayer, but she'd kept off any excess weight and she moved gracefully. Much of the tension I'd noted earlier had fallen away. I asked about her health.

"I've started swimming at a low-key, uncrowded health club. The arthritis is still there, but working with Lawry, I can be careful not to overdo it. I'm more relaxed all the time. We've patterned our lives to be more healthy for both of us. Living here means we take more walks. Also, we love taking classes at the New School, and I can teach in the neighborhood.

"Yes, I'm pleased with the choices I've made. I'm better at letting go of things than I used to be. I'd like to be absolutely certain that Lawry would never have another heart attack, but of course that isn't possible. In Al-Anon people talk about taking life 'one day at a time.' After all these years, I finally know how. I try to enjoy every moment!"

CAROLE'S OPPORTUNITY KNOCKED

I arranged to take time on my vacation to track down Carole in Paris last summer. She looked fabulous, and had a tall, lanky Frenchman on her arm. "My sister introduced us," she said of Jean-Paul. She too had a certain serenity.

As we settled into a café near the Louvre, she said, "My international assignment is still evolving." Though still with the same company, she was now a marketing vice president for a new series of financial products.

"I love it here—the pace, sophistication, the language. They think I'm exotic," she laughed. She returned to the United States for business several times a year and visited her sister Sarah in Racine. "Ro got married and moved to Geneva, but we're still very close. We meet for vacations near her whenever I can get away. Jean-Paul's restaurant is closed in August, so we go to the mountains or beach then too. This year, though, we want to go to Africa. We'll be linking up with a group of ten or twelve black kids from all over the United States. I'll be a sort of mentor to them. We'll all be exploring our roots, and seeing some wild animals too. An angel made all this possible!" She looked at Jean-Paul and winked.

"Everything has come together. My life today is a synthesis of the dreams and the plans I had earlier." Learner that she was, she made it all happen.

DIANA'S STORY REWRITTEN

Diana seemed settled in her small but growing company. Her former consumer products company was acquired by a German conglomerate after she left. "The culture has changed and I'm so glad I left when I did. Many corporations have cut their communication staffs, so we get their business. We now do video annual reports, not only for corporations, but as marketing tools for investment banks and law partnerships as well." She showed me their glossy printed pieces attractively packaged alongside their video tie-ins.

"Naturally, I enjoy meeting with the people with whom we work. I never thought of myself as a high-tech sort of person, but I keep learning."

She escaped the hectic pace every evening and got up early every morning to write or simply be alone in her attic nook in Park Slope. She showed me current photos of Kimmy in a princess costume for a school play and Jason as a Cub Scout in the Catskills. "They're still a handful, but we manage."

ELINOR'S ADVENTURE CONTINUES

I arranged to meet Elinor at the office of one of her vendors and talk with her during her lunch break. Since she stopped smoking, she had added a few pounds and curves to her slender frame. Chic as ever, she was a little softer looking.

She explained that she had met her new business partner on a trip to Scandinavia. An importer too, he appreciated her creative flair and her eye for trends. She liked his attention to details and planning abilities. They joined forces and were carefully building their business, selling to established stores, before launching their own.

"Plan A is under way. Remember, I was going to start my own importing company with sources I've discovered in India, Nepal, South America. Well, I've built a reputation in the craft and designer markets by contracting with native artisans around the world for original crafts. I've been expanding my price points higher and lower on best sellers. I love working with the crafts people, mostly women, and they're ecstatic about selling their things. I see that they get a fair price and I earn a good markup too." Still energetic and not afraid of risks, she calculated her moves more carefully now.

"As for the next step, I hope to buy a building in Loisada [Manhattan's Lower East Side] with my partner. My father might put some money into it too. I'd have a retail outlet on the ground floor, live in the top-floor loft and have myself a jungle on the roof! Others have done it, and so will I!"

She spoke excitedly. "We've got these great Malaysian fabrics for a new line of wrapables. I'm testing them, but one of the big stores wants them first. We picked up a number of new accounts this year." She was obviously enjoying her early successes.

"I feel like an explorer—a new Marco Polo, a twenty-first-century trader in search of adventure and profit!" She whizzed off to Macy's to meet with her former assistant. "He could be a really big customer too," she confided as she ran her lacquered acrylic nails through her auburn hair. Although not as far along as the others, she'd come a long way and she wasn't yet thirty. I have great hopes for her.

Explorer, pioneer of a generation or the universe, you're on your own journey now. You've charted your course, keeping in mind not only your itinerary but the quality of the journey and the people you want to travel with you. Whatever happens, whatever narrow straits you may encounter, your willingness to learn will lead you ahead to where you want to be, whether it's to greater safety or greater adventure.

As women of the late twentieth century, we're pioneers who've discovered and claimed a long-lost birthright, taking many risks as we endeavor to define ourselves as more than wives, mothers, daughters and even professionals. We are heroines with a thousand faces, a thousand challenges, each creating our own epic as we learn our way through life.

Bon voyage! Do send a postcard now and then as you pause in your travels. Reactions, comments, ideas for another book? Send them all to me, Dr. Betsy Jaffe, Career Continuum, 7 West 14th St., P.O. Box 20-FS, New York, NY 10011. May the road rise up to meet you and the wind be at your back. Thanks for taking me along at least part of the way.

Additional Resources

BOOKS

Introduction—Seeing the Big Picture

Age Wave, Ken Dychtwald, Ph.D., Jeremy P. Tarcher, Inc., 1989.
Falling from Grace, Katherine S. Newman, The Free Press, 1988.
Information Anxiety, Richard Saul Wurman, Doubleday, 1989.
The Hunger for More, Laurence Shames, Time Books, 1989.
The Sisterhood, Marcia Cohen, Simon & Schuster, 1988.

PART I—COPING WITH CHANGE

Chapter I—Lives in Crisis—Yours and Theirs

Breaking the Glass Ceiling, Ann Morrison, Randall White and Ellen Van Velson, Center for Creative Leadership, 1987.
Lifeprints: New Patterns of Love and Work for Today's Woman, Grace Baruch, Rosalind Barnett and Caryl Rivers, McGraw-Hill, 1983.
Management Women's Life Transitions, Elizabeth Latimer Jaffe, University Microfilms International, 1985.
Women MBAs, A Foot in the Door, Mary D. Fillmore, G. K. Hall & Co., 1987.

Chapter II—Five Coping Styles

Managing with Style, Alan Rowe and Richard Mason, Jossey-Bass, 1987.
The Creative Brain, Ned Herrmann, Brain Books, 1988.
Type Talk, Otto Kroeger and Janet Thuesen, Delacorte Press, 1988.

Chapter III—Tapping Your Resources

Among Friends, Letty Cottin Pogrebin, McGraw-Hill, 1986.
Overwhelmed: Coping with Life's Ups and Downs, Nancy K. Schlossberg, Lexington Books, 1989.

Staying on Top, Kathryn D. Cramer, Viking, 1990.
Tradeoffs, Barrie Greiff and Preston Munter, New American Library, 1981.
When Smart People Fail: Rebuilding Yourself for Success, Carole Hyatt and Linda Gottlieb, Simon & Schuster, 1987.
Women Analyze Women, Elaine Baruch and Lucienne Serrano, NYU Press, 1989.

PART II—SHAPING YOUR LIFE

Chapter IV—New Shapes in Careers

Managerial Lives in Transition, Ann Howard and Douglas Bray, Guilford Publications, 1989.
Managing the New Careerists, Brooklyn Derr, Jossey-Bass, 1986.
Pack Your Own Chute, Paul Hirsch, Addison-Wesley, 1987.
The Lessons of Experience, Morgan McCall, Michael Lombard and Ann Morrison, Lexington Books, 1989.

Chapter V—Your Roles, Relationships and Balance

Black Sheep and Kissing Cousins, How Our Family Stories Shape Us, Elizabeth Stone, Times Books, 1988.
Lifemates, Harold Bloomfield and Sirah Vettese with Robert Kory, New American Library, 1989.
Maternal Thinking, Sara Ruddick, Beacon Press, 1989.
Remaking Motherhood, Anita Shreve, Fawcett, 1987.
Second Chances, Judith Wallerstein and Sandra Blakeslee, Ticknor & Fields, 1989.
The Power of the Family, Paula Pearsall, Doubleday, 1990.
The Second Shift, Arlie Hochschild with Anne Machung, Viking, 1989.
You Can't Do It All, Irvina Siegel Lew, Berkley, 1987.

Chapter VI—Your Ambitions and Your Health

Jane Brody's The New York Times Guide to Personal Health, Avon Books, 1982.
Children of Alcoholism: Struggle for Self & Intimacy in Adult Life, Barbara Wood, NYU Press, 1987.
Smoke Screen, Betsy Tice White, Abingdon Press, 1989.
Stress Map, Personal Diary Edition, Esther Orioli, Dennis Jaffe and Cynthia Scott, Newmarket Press, 1987.
The Mind, Richard Restak, Bantam Books, 1988.
The Physician Within, Catherine Fente, Diabetes Center, 1987.
The New Our Bodies, Ourselves, The Boston Women's Health Book Collective, Touchstone, 1984.

We Are Not Alone: Learning to Live With Chronic Illness, Sfra Kobrin Pityele, Workman, 1989.

PART III—PLANNING YOUR FUTURE

Chapter VII—Career-Building Competencies

Competition in Global Industries, Michael Porter, Harvard Business School, 1986.
Developing Critical Thinkers, Stephen Brookfield, Jossey-Bass, 1987.
Encounters with the Future, Marvin Cetron and Owen Davis, Simon & Schuster, 1988.
Future Perfect, Stan Davis, Addison-Wesley, 1987.

Chapter VIII—To Change or Not to Change?

Going to Work, Lisa Birnbach, Villard Books, 1988.
How to Make It Big as a Consultant, William Cohen, AMACOM, 1985.
Marketing Your Consulting and Professional Services, Richard Connor and Jeffrey Davidson, John Wiley & Sons, 1985.
Running a One Person Business, Claude Whitmeyer, Salli Rasberry and Michael Phillips, Ten Speed Press, 1989.
The Best Companies for Women, Baila Zeitz and Lorraine Dusky, Simon and Schuster, 1988.
Working Together, Frank and Sharan Barnett, Ten Speed Press, 1988.

Chapter IX—Putting It All Together

Better Resumes for Executives & Professionals, Robert Wilson and Adele Lewis, Barron's, 1983.
Composing a Life, Mary Catherine Bateson, Atlantic Monthly Press, 1989.
Out-Interviewing the Interviewer, Stephen Merman and John McLaughlin, A Spectrum Book, 1983.
Self-Assessment and Career Development, James Clawson, John Kotter, Victor Faux and Charles McArthur, Prentice-Hall, 1985.
What Color Is Your Parachute, Richard Bolles, Ten Speed Press, 1990.
Women Making It, Patterns and Profiles of Success, Ruth Halcomb, Atheneum, 1979.
*The starred books are how-to career books.

ORGANIZATIONS

AARP, 1901 K St. N.W., Washington, DC 20049.
ACTION, Washington, DC 20525.

Big Sister of America, 230 N. 13th St., Philadelphia, PA 19107.

Catalyst, 250 Park Ave. S., New York, NY 10005.

Center for Creative Leadership, P.O. Box P-1, Greensboro, NC 27402.

Herrman—Applied Creative Services, 2075 Buffalo Creek Rd., Lake Lure, NC 28746.

NTL Institute, 1240 N. Pitt St., Suite 100, Alexandria, VA 22314-1403.

RESOLVE, 5 Water St., Dept. J, Arlington, MA 02174.

Small Business Administration, Office of Women's Business Ownership, 1441 L Street N.W. Washington, DC 20416.

Synectics Corp., 17 Dunster St., Cambridge, MA 02138.

Volunteer—The National Center, 1216 16th St. N.W., Washington, DC 20036.

Early Work, School and Life Experiences: Teens and Early Twenties

No matter what your age, you've already had disappointments, altered ambitions too—perhaps about schools you could attend, subjects you could major in, clubs, friends, that special someone, a physical or mental limitation. In *Altered Ambitions*, Chapter III, from the Steps to Take in a Crisis section to the end of the chapter are many coping strategies helpful to any age. School counselors and friends can suggest others.

One additional perspective is useful for young people, though—the meaning of the word "adult."

First of all, you may believe that school is not related to the "real" world. But in school, you're picking up skills in meeting deadlines, producing quality work, relating to authority figures and peers from different backgrounds. You're also learning to learn, while acquiring useful language, writing and communication skills, as well as technical skills. Perhaps most important of all, you're developing an understanding of human behavior.

In school, you have an opportunity to test your leadership skills and overcome shyness. You can learn to take responsibility for your behavior and your life, getting experience in dealing with new emotions and adult problems. Here you can become the best you can be, even if your family life, school or college isn't the best.

What *really* makes the difference in your road to adulthood, though, is experiencing those major life events and situations that are difficult: a retarded sibling, parental death or divorce, any unexpected setback that's "not fair"—those things unique to *your* life. Each of us is dealt our own assorted package of these in a lifetime. We learn from these events, and can grow to maturity and wisdom as we master the changes they trigger.

Try to look at these events as a way of being tested or an opportunity to use your problem-solving and coping skills. You've seen adults who don't cope very well. You can be different. Choose role models who seem to have it together, who are calm and responsible in a crisis, caring for others and confident in themselves. Seek them out, watch what they do and ask for their advice.

Those who best survive the most disastrous of childhoods are those who've been independent and self-sufficient enough to reach out for the help of caring adults. They can ease your way through the "growing pains" life hands us at every age. Who are your helpers?

EXERCISE

YOUR SUPPORT SYSTEM

1. In thinking about your life up to now, what have been your major life events? Events that changed how you thought of yourself and others? After which you said, "I'm different now." Jot down each event you remember:

A._____

B._____

C._____

D._____

E._____

Use other paper if you need it.

2. Who were the people who helped you get through those events? Write down their names.

Event A._____   _____   _____

       B._____   _____   _____

C._____   _____   _____

D._____   _____   _____

E._____   _____   _____

These people are your support system.

3. Who would you like to add to this list? Who might you like as a future adviser? Write down their names. _____

_____

Get to know them better. Seek their advice on the problems you have now; don't wait for a crisis.

Although *Altered Ambitions* is written primarily for working women, the information here can be very useful whatever your gender or age. For those only now beginning to form ambitions and dreams of the future, no one knows what the world will be like. All we can say for certain is that it will be different from the world of today. That is, after all, the real reason I undertook this book.

Index